Philip Roth Studies is produced in cooperation with the Philip Roth Society and is a member of the Council of Editors of Learned Journals.

David Brauner and Debra Shostak
Executive Co-Editors

Jessica G. Rabin
Associate Editor

Jacques Berlinerblau
Book Review Editor

Derek Parker Royal
Founder and Former Executive Editor

ADVISORY BOARD

Victoria Aarons
Trinity University

James Bloom
Muhlenberg College

David Gooblar
University of Iowa

Sandor Goodhart
Purdue University

Jay L. Halio
University of Delaware

Patrick Hayes
University of Oxford

Pia Masiero
Ca' Foscari University of Venice

Brian McDonald
Adelphi University

Catherine Morley
University of Leicester

Ira B. Nadel
University of British Columbia

Gurumurthy Neelakantan
Indian Institute of Technology, Kanpur

Patrick O'Donnell
Michigan State University

Ranen Omer-Sherman
University of Louisville

Timothy Parrish
University of California, Davis

Aimee Pozorski
Central Connecticut State University

Maren Scheurer
Goethe-Universität Frankfurt am Main

James A. Schiff
University of Cincinnati

George Searles
Mohawk Valley Community College

Ruth Knafo Setton
Lehigh University

Matthew Shipe
Washington University in St. Louis

Hana Wirth-Nesher
Tel Aviv University

SUBSCRIPTIONS

For subscription information, contact:

    Purdue University Press c/o Baker & Taylor Publisher Services
    Phone: 1-800-247-6553; Fax: 1-419-281-6883
    E-mail: order@btpublisherservices.com

SUBMISSIONS

The journal welcomes full-length articles as well as shorter notes. Articles should be between 5,000 and 10,000 words in length, and notes should not exceed 2,500 words. A brief abstract (approximately 50 words) should accompany each submission. Manuscripts and book reviews must be prepared according to the *MLA Handbook, 8th ed.* (2016), and should contain endnotes rather than footnotes. All submissions must be sent via e-mail as an attached document. Please address all submissions and queries to the executive co-editors, David Brauner and Debra Shostak, at philiprothstudies@gmail.com.

Articles appearing in this journal are indexed in the *Humanities International Complete, Index to Jewish Periodicals, MLA International Bibliography, Project Muse,* and *Scopus.*

Print ISSN: 1547-3929
Electronic ISSN: 1940-5278
ISBN: 978-1-55753-878-9

Cover image: Adaptation of watercolor of Philip Roth by J. C. Phillipps.

PHILIP ROTH
STUDIES

VOLUME 15, NO. 1 • CONTENTS
SPECIAL MEMORIAL ISSUE

Contents

Abbreviations

The following abbreviations for Roth's works appear within parenthetical citations. Listed below as *Title [Abbreviation]*, abbreviations appear in order of publication date.

NOVELS/NOVELLAS

Goodbye, Columbus and Five Short Stories [Goodbye]
Letting Go [Letting Go]
When She Was Good [WSWG]
Portnoy's Complaint [Portnoy]
Our Gang [Gang]
The Breast [Breast]
The Great American Novel [GAN]
My Life as a Man [My Life]
The Professor of Desire [Professor]
The Ghost Writer [Ghost]
Zuckerman Unbound [Unbound]
The Anatomy Lesson [Anatomy]
The Prague Orgy [Prague]
Zuckerman Bound [Bound]
The Counterlife [Counterlife]
The Facts: A Novelist's Autobiography [Facts]
Deception: A Novel [Deception]
Patrimony: A True Story [Patrimony]
Operation Shylock: A Confession [Shylock]
Sabbath's Theater [Sabbath]
American Pastoral [Pastoral]
I Married a Communist [Communist]
The Human Stain [Stain]
The Dying Animal [Dying]
The Plot Against America [Plot]
Everyman [Everyman]
Exit Ghost [Exit]
Indignation [Indignation]
The Humbling [Humbling]
Nemesis [Nemesis]

NONFICTION COLLECTIONS

Reading Myself and Others [Reading]
Shop Talk: A Writer and His Colleagues and Their Work [Shop]
Why Write? Collected Nonfiction 1960–2013 [Why Write?]

NOTE

Editors' Note

David Brauner and
Debra Shostak

There is a certain symmetry to the fact that our last issue as Executive Co-Editors is also the issue in which we bid farewell to Roth the man. It also coincides with the news that the journal has been accepted by Elsevier's Scopus, the largest abstract and citation database of peer-reviewed literature, a gratifying endorsement of the status of *Philip Roth Studies* in the wider academic community. So for us this special memorial issue is an opportunity to reflect not just on everything that Roth has meant to us over the course of our careers, but also on the place the journal itself has occupied in our lives over the past five years. In doing so, we want to express our gratitude to all the folks at Purdue University Press, particularly Katherine Purple, our production manager, whose professionalism and efficiency during our term of office has been exemplary; to our Editorial Board, whose careful reviewing of submissions has helped maintain the standards of the journal; to Jacques Berlinerblau, our ebullient book editor; to our diligent, eagle-eyed Associate Editor and Managing Editor, Jessica Rabin and Christopher Gonzalez; to the officers of the Roth Society; and most of all, to you, our subscribers and readers. We would also like to take this opportunity to pay tribute to Andrew Gordon, who has lately passed away. A highly-valued member of the community of Roth scholars, Andy published a number of essays for us over the years. We will miss him.

We are particularly pleased that this special memorial issue is our swan song because we think it captures beautifully what distinguishes Roth's writing: his audacity, fearlessness, and fierce intelligence; his stylistic brilliance, formal adventurousness, and ethical rigor; above all, perhaps, his aesthetic integrity—his fidelity to his own values as a writer. What struck us most forcefully, reading this wonderful collection of tributes from scholars young and not so young, established and emerging, is the peculiarly tenacious hold that Roth has exerted over our imaginations, the sense of intimacy and personal investment that his work has generated. He has had a profound impact on our personal as well as our professional lives; he has pervaded our consciousnesses and spoken to us in our dreams. We have been inspired by his work to treat that work with an irreverent reverence and reverent irreverence. Last but not least, we are very proud that this issue features the final interview with Roth, conducted by Elèna Mortara.

Roth may be dead but his works live on and we are confident that *Philip Roth Studies* will continue to thrive under the stewardship of Aimee Pozorski and Maren Scheurer. Aimee is of course one of the leading scholars in the field and Maren has published innovative and exciting work on Roth in recent years, not least in this journal. Together, they co-edited another recent special issue of the journal, so they already know the ropes. We wish them all the best for the future, happy in the knowledge that the journal couldn't be in better hands.

ARTICLE

Philip Roth, December 2017

A Meeting and an Interview*

Interview conducted by Elèna Mortara

A sunny winter day in New York, December 21, 2017. Shining sun, clear blue sky, and a pleasantly whipping wind: I'm walking in the Upper West Side of Manhattan towards my appointment with Philip Roth. Two months have passed since the publication in Italy of the first volume of Philip Roth's fiction in the most prestigious Italian literary series, *Meridiani Mondadori* (the Italian equivalent of the *Library of America* edition in the U.S.A. and *La Pléiade* by Gallimard in France): a leather-bound critical edition of about two thousand pages, including eight of his novels, 1959-1986, edited by me. And now I am on my way to meet with him in his apartment. At the entrance of the elegant multi-floor building close to the American Museum of Natural History and Central Park where he lives, there are some comfortable condominium armchairs, but I don't need to wait because the doorman immediately calls upstairs and announces my arrival. Up on the twelfth floor, near the threshold, just outside his open door, there is Philip Roth, welcoming me. When I enter, I am flooded with the light of the bright and spacious living room, with large balcony-windows over the opposite wall open to the sight of the city. Roth is wearing a slate-blue shirt and brown wool trousers. We sit in this light-flooded space, with a low table filled with books next to us, and start our conversation.

It's a friendly conversation, moving from memories of his experience in Rome as a young man to family recollections, from his encounters with other writers to reflections on his books. There are moments of great laughter and sometimes surprising discoveries to be made in this conversation. Roth is not

*"Philip Roth, December 2017: A Meeting and an Interview," interview by Elèna Mortara Copyright © 2017 Philip Roth, used by permission of the Wylie Agency LLC.

only welcoming, but also looks in great shape. "I'm happy," he admits with all simplicity, when I ask him how he feels, now that he has just published a new splendid collection of essays (*Why Write?*, 2017) in the United States, while simultaneously in Europe the two most important literary series in Italy and France have independently started the publication of their prestigious critical collections of most of his fiction in their Pantheons, beginning, by some mysterious coincidence, at exactly the same time: October 2017. There appears to be an amazing simultaneous celebration, a sort of double Nobel Prize in Literature being awarded to Roth by these two European countries. Yet this is a thought I keep to myself, preferring not to touch on this awkward subject. I ask him why he requested Gallimard to revise their previous French translations of his books, while he insisted on keeping the existing Italian translations in our Mondadori edition. It's because the Italian translations were already good, he explains to me, while all his friends in France had told him that the French ones were not so good. We then start talking about his still probably most famous novel, the one that revolutionized American literature and his career, *Portnoy's Complaint*, in whose title the word "complaint" creates all sorts of problems for translators in all languages. "*Lamento,*" he suddenly remarks, pronouncing the Italian word with a surprisingly good accent, "is not perfect," and he begins to explain the reasons for his perplexity. I wish to remember his precise words on such an important subject, so that's when I decide, with his agreement, to start recording our conversation.

Elèna Mortara: We were talking about the word *Complaint* in the title of your *Portnoy's Complaint*, which in Italian is translated as *Lamento di Portnoy*. What can you say about the meanings of that key-word?

Philip Roth: When I wrote "*Complaint,*" what I was thinking of were two things. One is *a lover's complaint*, which is a phrase that you can use for certain English seventeenth-century poetry: a lover addresses his complaint to his beloved, who doesn't love him back in return. And secondly, as *an illness: complaint*. In the beginning of the book I have a definition of the illness. So, in the beginning of the book what do they do in the Italian edition when they have that definition, they don't say "*lamento,*" do they?

EM: No. Do you remember the word you use at the beginning in that definition of the illness? You don't repeat "complaint," you use another word, which is "*disorder.*" In the Italian translation they say "*disturbo,*" which corresponds to the word you also use. So it means a kind of illness, which can also be psychological, of course.

PR: Good. That's ok.

EM: But it is impossible to find one word that has all these meanings that you have in the English word "complaint." So what I remarked in my introduction somewhere, or in my commentary on *Portnoy's Complaint*, is that in *all* languages you have a different translation, which only covers one part of the meaning. And you are stressing the poetic meaning of the word "complaint" . . .

PR: I'm stressing both.

EM: There is also another meaning, which is not poetic but judicial.

PR: Oh yes, you file a complaint, with the court.

EM: When you are referring to the poetic connotation of this word, who are you thinking of? Who was the beloved? Please explain what you meant!

PR: In *Portnoy's Complaint,* the beloved is his mother! Yah, it's a kind of love poem! But it also means "to complain" in the obvious sense. He complains all the time.

EM: Yes, but the fact that this is a love poem has never been said or written before! I think that's wonderful!

KAFKA

EM: Now, I would like to start the more formal part of our conversation with this question: Why did you decide to have "'I Always Wanted You to Admire My Fasting'; or, Looking at Kafka" as the first piece of your new wonderful collection, *Why Write?*

PR: Because I like it so much! It was a gift to me. I was teaching at the University of Pennsylvania in the 1970s, early '70s, I was teaching a course on Kafka and I had this wonderful class, they were so smart. And so I was going to write this biographical piece about Kafka for the class. And then, while I was writing it, I just got this idea for Kafka as my Hebrew school teacher. Because I went to Hebrew school after school, it was after school. I hated it.

EM: I remember what you have written about that!

PR: I mean I'm glad I did it, but . . . and what I knew of it! And the teachers, some of them, were refugees. That's where I got the idea, because we had these refugees, these tormented poor guys, you know. All of us Jewish boys were perfect in regular school and mischievous in Hebrew school.

EM: In the Preface of *Why Write?*, when you talk about this story you call it a "hybrid essay story." So isn't it also a way of starting your collection of essays by reminding us that you are a fiction writer, stressing the hybrid quality of this text?

PR: Yes, and the book ends in that way too. The last piece ends with that long piece from *Sabbath's Theater*.

EM: That's right, so you created a frame.

PR: That's right.

EM: To remind readers that you are, yes, writing essays, I must say wonderful essays, but at the same time you are a fiction writer. I felt this way. Do you agree?

PR: Yes, I do.

EM: And at the same time you are stressing the importance that Kafka has had for you. I don't know if you want to say something about this.

PR: Well, I only really studied, I read Kafka in my twenties, I did not know what it was, really. But then in my thirties, I began to read Kafka again and I got it, I understood it, I felt the force of it, and the majesty of it, really. And so I began to teach Kafka, and then I got so close to it in teaching Kafka. And then I went to Prague, actually the first time just as a kind of pilgrim, you know. Subsequently I met all these Czech writers. But I went there at the beginning just to see Kafka's city . . . My book *The Professor of Desire* has a nice scene, where someone is introduced to Kafka's prostitute. Do you remember that?

EM: Yes, of course!

PR: That's a very nice scene! She says, as I remember, she says: "You never hit me. Why don't Jewish boys ever hit me?"

EM: But, as a writer, in what way did Kafka influence you, or impress you?

PR: Well, the obsessiveness, the obsessiveness. The working of a situation in every aspect, turning a situation over and over and over. The comedy too. And then the dramatization of ultimate frustration, the dramatization of ultimate entrapment. That all spoke to me at that point. So I don't write like Kafka, of course . . . And the mind that comes through, the mind behind it. It's so interesting, his mind is hidden, the mind is hidden, but it's there.

EM: And it comes out in his journals, I love his journals.

PR: Yes, his journals are wonderful.

EM: I remember that in that essay-story about Kafka at a certain point you speak about a family association of two hundred people. Is this something that comes from reality, from your real experience?

PR: (*Rising*): You can get up? I'll show you a picture.

EM: (*Rising too*): Yah, let me see . . . O-Oh, wonderful! Oh, well, really . . . !

PR: (*Showing a photograph that was hanging on the wall—with about 150 people sitting at long tables in an elegant dining room*): Let me see if I can find my family. Oh, there is my mother! This is my mother. And where is my father? . . . Here he is!

EM: Oh. Can I take a picture of this?

PR: Yes, of course!

EM: And this was not all family . . .

PR: Yes, all family! Family on my paternal grandmother's side.

EM: Oh, that's incredible!

PR: Yes, this was very common in America, in the 1920s. The Jewish families, they had a right to leave between 1880 and 1900. And the first generation struggled, but their children, who had a step up, who were more middle class, formed these family associations. They were very common among Jews. They were kind of welfare societies, they would loan money for burials, if someone was sick, they had a scholarship fund for kids going to college, who didn't happen to have money. And then there was great family feeling among them. I, as a little child, I loved going; when I was a little one, I loved going. I think by the time this one was taken, I was too sophisticated!

EM: This picture was taken in 1949.

PR: 1949. I would have been sixteen. I was too old.

EM: That was the age of rebellion, the beginning of the age of rebellion.

PR: Yes . . .

EM: And they were all related, you mean . . . !?

PR: They were all related, on my paternal grandmother's side. It's really my grandmother's mother's family: some matriarchy. I think my grandmother should be in there, let me see if I can find her. She would be at the head of the table, yah . . . There she is! There she is, little grandma!

EM: (*Moved*): The one you would go and see . . .

PR: That's my father's mother, and we would go see them every Sunday morning, in Newark, in a poor section, . . . she lived in a poor section of Newark.

EM: Yes, the one where your father grew up?

PR: Yes, where my father grew up. So every Sunday morning we went there, and every Sunday afternoon we went to my mother's mother. Our grandfathers had died: one before I was born, after whom I was named, and one when I was about seven years old, whom I have only the dimmest memory of. But the grandmothers I had a strong connection to. But they spoke only Yiddish.

EM: Both of them?

PR: Well, my mother's mother spoke some English. My father's mother spoke very little English. She'd been busy at home having babies, she didn't get out into the world, you know. Yes, but, you know, the intensity of the feeling was magnified by not being able to communicate. You burst in to say something. Yes, I loved them both, yah.

EM: And I think, if I remember correctly, that to go to your grandmothers' homes you had to cross a cemetery . . .

PR: That's right!

EM: This may have had some influence, because of the many cemetery scenes in your fiction!

PR: I hated passing that cemetery, it scared me, you know. And during the war, when gas was rationed, so we only had so much gas for the car a week, my father needed the car for work, so on the Sundays we would walk. So we had to walk past the cemetery. It was bad enough to drive past the cemetery. Yes, you remember that cemetery! I do have a lot of cemetery scenes.

EM: And so, is that something that was in the background of your mind, when that came up later in your fiction?

PR: No, it wasn't. I don't know how that happened. I think it happened when I began to go to funerals all the time. I guess when I turned … my mid-sixties. My friends who were fifteen years older than I was, or twenty, began to die, I began to go to funerals all the time, you know.

FIRST DEDICATION AND NEIGHBORHOOD

EM: I have noticed that your first dedication in your first book, *Goodbye, Columbus*, is to your mother and father, which is something that critics have not noticed so much, particularly at the beginning of your career, when they started criticizing your approach. They didn't realize the importance of that dedication. In your introduction to your book of essays you quote and emphasize the sentence by Edna O'Brien, "The defining influences on him are his parents." I have noticed the importance of this influence and of the dedication. I wonder if you agree.

PR: You know, my parents, they were very important to me, because they were so good and raised my brother and me with such warmth and love. But also the community where I grew up, that neighborhood, was a big neighborhood, Jewish neighborhood, was like a larger parent. Because they were all Jews, there were a few Gentile families, but not very many. I guess I was speaking to one of my old high-school friends on the phone, he lives in Florida, and we speak once in a while, and he said to me about Weequahic, our neighborhood: "It was so safe," he said, "we felt so safe." And we really felt so safe.

EM: In dangerous times, it was safe.

PR: During the war, America wasn't in danger, but we had absorbed the war, and it was so safe. And also we knew about antisemitism, because in the thirties the United States was a very antisemitic country, very much so, in the twenties and thirties in America. And then of course we knew about Hitler. So we knew that there were places where we were despised. Yet in this place we were loved, there was a kind of communal love. So it was a very special place, a very special place.

EM: In one of your essays, you speak about yourself at a certain point as a "schmaltz man," I love that self-definition of yours. You say, "in matters Goldenian, I am a schmaltz man myself."

PR: Yes, that's Harry Golden, who was full of schmaltz, you know. I was being sarcastic.

EM: Sarcastic? So this leads me to a series of questions. First of all . . . I feel that for you Jewishness has been very important, not Judaism as a system of thought, as a religion, but Jewishness, the experience of being a Jew.

PR: Yes, ethnic Judaism we might say. Sure, because I was always aware of myself as a Jew, though I was never observant. I was bar-mitzvahed, that was the last time I went to a synagogue. The historical predicament of Jews became clear to me very early. So I always was aware of it. As far as the choices of my people in my books, I wrote about them because I knew about them. I was interested in Jews, I was interested in these people I knew, they were Jews, you know. And after my first book, after *Goodbye, Columbus*, except for *Portnoy's Complaint*, if you take out *Goodbye, Columbus* and *Portnoy's Complaint*, the whole importance of Jewishness diminishes. It's nowhere in my trilogy, *American Pastoral*. He is Jewish, but . . .

EM: Well, I would say that there are other books where it is extremely important. One is *The Counterlife.*

PR: Oh yes, yes. That's about Israel.

EM: Then *The Plot Against America.*

PR: Oh yes, you are right! But from a different perspective than in the first, than in *Portnoy's Complaint* and in *Goodbye, Columbus*. It becomes historicized and politicized, in *The Plot Against America.*

EM: And in *The Counterlife* you show the debate.

PR: Yes.

EM: And then there is of course *Operation Shylock*. There are many books, where you still . . .

PR: I can't get out from under it!

ZUCKERMAN'S NAME AND BEGINNING OF THE SERIES

EM: No, you can't! Anyhow, talking about you as a *schmaltz* man in a sardonic way, this leads me to the question about Zuckerman: the choice of this name. How did you decide about this name, which you first introduced in *My Life as a Man*?

PR: Yes, that was a false end there. To begin with, I didn't dream I was going to write nine books. It just seemed like I was going to write *The Ghost Writer*.

EM: Oh, really? When you started, you only thought you would write *The Ghost Writer*?

PR: Well, that's complicated. When I started, I wrote a big book, a first draft, very rough: what became the first four books, *The Ghost Writer* down to *The Prague Orgy*. That was all one book. In fact, the focus was on Prague, and always the contrast backward. And it was very bad, and I thought: you're trying to do too much, take it apart. So it is correct to say I was going to write only one book. But I didn't think it was going to be a useful character forever. And the name, it was a name that was known in my neighborhood. Yes, Zuckerman. I went to school with a boy named Leo Zuckerman. He felt very amused (if he is still alive . . .). It was not an uncommon Jewish name. But I don't like the common, I always try to find some name that isn't common, a Jewish name that is not common.

EM: I feel, maybe because of the importance of this character, that there is more in this name. And you explain the fact of using a name with some sweetness in it in *The Ghost Writer*, when you introduce an explanation for Amy Bellette's sweet name: she explains why she has chosen to hide under a sweet name. And I thought this was a way for you as the author to reflect on the choice of having this sweet name for Zuckerman, which is related to sugar (*Zucker*).

PR: Yes, of course.

EM: And at the same time — I don't know if you can agree with these series of explanations I'm giving to myself — when there is sweetness, and at the same time, Zuck . . . , "ck," the same sound of "Eric Duncan" (*Roth laughing loudly!*), so there is the conflict between the sweetness of the meaning and the hard quality of the "k." So I felt that you sort of fell in love with this name. I don't know if it was something subconscious, that you didn't so much think about.

PR: I don't think that it was totally conscious. I did know a man named Sugar, of course, because I went to college with a guy named Sugarman, a fellow named Nate Sugarman. And I thought of his name, using his name, I now remember. But that was too obvious.

EM: So that was a name with the English word "*Sugar*," not "*Zucker*."

PR: Yah, his name was Sugarman. And I thought of using his name. And I thought: it's too much on the nose.

EM: So you chose the Yiddish version of the name.

PR: Yah.

ITALY, THE WAR, ITALIAN WRITERS AND ENCOUNTERS

EM: Now, I would like you to talk about Italy, your Italian experience, actually your many Italian experiences, since you have had several, and the way Italy is present in your books.

PR: Is Italy present in my books?

EM: Yes, that's something that has never been noticed, I think.

PR: I don't even notice it! Can you tell me in which books?

EM: Well, in *Portnoy's Complaint*, there are the Via Veneto scenes . . .

PR: Oh, yes.

EM: In *The Ghost Writer*, there are Siena and—

PR: Florence . . .

EM: . . . and Florence, which are there as dream places for Amy Bellette, who would like to escape with Lonoff. So Italy is associated with fun, allurement, and with dream, as a place of beauty, on the one hand. On the other hand, you mention Italy a lot in *Sabbath's Theater* . . .

PR: Oh yes, Sabbath goes to puppets' school!

EM: He goes to puppets' school there. And I noticed a difference in this novel, because you seem to know about the war, the experience of the war in Italy. It's no longer only the place of tourism, of dreams, of rather artificial references, which are more common among writers when speaking about this country, but, maybe because of your experience at the end of the fifties when you came to Italy, you seem to know that in Italy there had been a war. And Sabbath mentions the war in Italian, he uses the Italian word for "war," "guerra," saying "*La guerra*" ("The war"), you put it there in the text. So I was wondering if you can say something more.

PR: You know, I made up that whole scene, the puppeteer, the puppet master, and the school, it's complete invention. I just thought Italy would be a good place for it, it was a kind of spontaneous selection. And I liked the puppet teacher, who says to him . . . he has a girl-friend who is 15-years-old, isn't that what he says to him?

EM: Yes, at a certain point he even says 13 or 12.

PR: "But I have known her since she was 12."

EM: Yes! So, what about your Italian experiences?

PR: Well, it's over fifty, sixty years ago, a little less than sixty years ago.

EM: That was first in 1958, when you won the Aga Kahn prize for fiction.

PR: Yes, that was the first time I went to Europe. The first time I went to Europe I was in Paris, and then I hitchhiked down to Florence. And I just did the things that a young fellow—I was twenty-five—a young fellow would do. I saw everything, you know, studiously saw everything. But that's what made me want to go back in 1959, that I wanted to see more of Italy. You know, at that time in America it was no longer Paris that was the place to go to. Rome was the place to go to.

EM: Why?

PR: I don't know, it had a certain glamour in the late fifties. And I knew some . . . my friend William Styron and his wife were there. I didn't know them until I went to Rome, there they were. . . Oh, I think I did know them! They stayed there for part of our time. Well, my life in Rome. We first went to Florence for a month. We stayed in a *pensione* near the Uffizi, I don't remember the name of the street, and for a month we stayed there. I would write during the mornings, and then the afternoons go out and walk around, I might be visiting Siena and so on. And then, going down to Rome, I don't remember how we got the apartment, we did. I loved the via Giulia, right outside the door, I loved living around the corner of that street. And we could see the river from our apartment, at the corner, you know. Though I was married, very unhappily (*laughing*), and my wife and I had arguments. We were both young, we had terrible arguments, even the Italians had never seen anything like it! Yes, yes, they came out on the landing and listened to the screaming that was going on upstairs!

EM: My mother always told us about when she came to Italy from Vienna, on the train there was a family and she was afraid something terrible was happening, because they were shouting and she didn't understand Italian at that time. But then she realized that it was just normal conversation! Do you know that my mother would speak Latin to the porter?

PR: Oh really?

EM: She would say: *"Impedimenta ante portas"* ("The luggage at the gates"), using her Latin from the ancient Roman warning against Hannibal (*"Hannibal ante portas"*) in Cicero and Titus Livy; that was funny. Anyhow, coming back to you . . .

PR: I know I was writing *Letting Go*, that's what I was doing. And I think I somehow wound up getting a studio, up at the American Academy: Janiculum, is that what it's called? Somebody had a studio and I began to use it. So I drove, I'd go up every morning. Yes, I had bought a little car, I think I drove. And I just remember, only one of the people I knew intimately was Italian. She was Anthony Burgess's wife, named Liana, Liana Burgess. Oh, excuse me. She was married first to my friend in Rome, an American black who fought with the black brigade in the American army in Italy, and after he was discharged, he took his discharge in Italy, he stayed there.

EM: And what's his name?

PR: Ben Johnson, his name was.

EM: Maybe that's how you knew about the war, I mean the war in Italy.

PR: No, I knew about the war in Italy from being a kid, when I was a kid. As a child, I was obsessed with World War II. My father talked about it, he brought the paper home every night. I would read the paper about World War II. I would worry about World War II. And I knew what happened, I knew the names of Anzio, I knew where the Americans had landed, I knew about the invasion of Sicily, I knew it all since I was a kid. So Ben introduced me to Italian literature.

EM: Oh!

PR: Because he was a translator. And so I began to read Carlo Levi, Moravia, Silone, not Primo Levi. And . . . Natalia Ginzburg, and the guy who wrote *The Garden of the Finzi-Continis* . . . ? Yes, Bassani, Giorgio Bassani. And so I began to read all these books.

EM: And did you meet any of them?

PR: I only met Moravia. He couldn't have cared less, I mean, he was very pompous. No, I didn't meet . . . I was nobody. You know, I was just an American *"kind"* there, I'd published one book. *Goodbye, Columbus* had been published before I went, but it had got very little attention. Only while I was *in* Italy it won the National Book Award, and I had to come back to America for a few days. But prior to that I was just somebody else who had written. No Italian journalist paid attention. It's just the way I was. So I had no Italian friendships. I remember the camaraderie, all these expatriates. There was a restaurant nearby, a little *trattoria,* and we went there practically every night, as did other friends, so we'd always be six or eight of us having dinner . . . Americans in Rome and English, Americans and English and Irish, yah. They were all writers.

EM: Did you ever meet Paolo Milano, who was a friend of Saul Bellow's and a critic? He was also a friend of mine.

PR: I think I met Paolo Milano in New York once, after, years after. I know he was Saul's friend, he cared about him.

EM: Yes, *The Victim* is . . .

PR: . . . dedicated to him, yah . . . No, I was just another obscure person.

EM: There are two Italian persons you met. I don't know if you remember the first one, whom you met at *Esquire,* when your first book had just been published, in 1959: Marisa Bulgheroni. You had just one brief meeting, I guess. She wrote an essay recollecting this meeting with you . . .

PR: Is that right!? What did she say!?

EM: She wrote very positively about the sense of, let's say, self-importance that she felt in you. I'm sorry that I don't have the text with me: it's in a new book of recollections of hers, *Chiamatemi Ismaele* (*Call Me Ishmael*), published in Italy in 2013. In 1959 she came to the States to write about contemporary American literature and, while she was ready to leave, someone told you that there was this Italian journalist. And so you had a meeting at *Esquire,* which she had not written about in her first book in the fifties, and she has recollected now in her new book. It's a wonderful essay about the meeting, where she describes you physically and writes about the impression she had, a very positive one.

PR: I would love to see it. Can you send me a copy of it? And I'll have my friend who speaks Italian . . .

EM: Of course, with great pleasure. Marisa Bulgheroni was one of my teachers at the University, and she was, and still is—for she is luckily still alive—a fascinating person. My main professor in American Studies at the University of Milan was Agostino Lombardo, a great professor, who had studied with Mario Praz, and became one of the main founders of American Studies in Italy after World War II, when the study of American literature was institutionalized for the first time in Italy. He was a wonderful teacher. And Marisa Bulgheroni also was very influential with us. So this is one Italian person you met in the States.

PR: And who is the other person I met?

EM: And then the second one is one of the interviewers that you have also kept in your new collection. It's Walter Mauro, remember?

PR: I don't remember. He is the first interviewer, one of the first, but I don't remember him.

EM: Reading Myself and Others begins with that interview. In fact, I wonder whether it was not a real meeting, but maybe a written exchange.

PR: It reads like a written exchange.

EM: I had this feeling, because, you know, I have what can be called the Italian "original," the book where he and his wife collected a series of interviews, which were about power, how writers dealt with power.

PR: Yes, that's what he was interested in.

EM: And he wanted to know from you how you had suffered from your parents! He didn't get the answer he wanted . . . ! And so, since in most of the other interviews he describes the place of the meeting, while there is no description of this kind as an introduction in your interview and he does not say *where* you met, so I felt that perhaps it was not a real meeting.

PR: I vaguely remember that we had a meeting, would have been here in America. And do you know him?

EM: Well, I met him once. He was a very important cultural journalist, and I met him not many years ago, in 2011, when I gave a talk at the Dante Alighieri Institute in Rome about Dante in the United States, and he was the chairperson of that talk. And so I met him, after reading him many times, and of course after knowing the interview that he had with you, which was an interview that you seemed to consider important, for you placed it at the beginning of your first collection.

PR: Well, I think in *Reading Myself and Others* it was chronological.

EM: No, it was not. You put it at the beginning without its being the first one, not at all. Because it was an interview of the Seventies, and of course you had other interviews before. No, it was not chronological. It's like with the Kafka. You decided that it was important.

PR: I have another old friend who is Italian, who lived in London and she became a friend of mine in London, it's Gaia Servadio. And we're dear friends. But I know her from living in London.

EM: And of course the other Italian person you met is Primo Levi.

PR: Yes, I met Primo, yah.

EM: I was moved by what you also say in your new introduction, when you talk about the dramatic effect of the news of his suicide on you, the inability to understand.

PR: I remember the day, because I was devastated like many people and I went to see Gaia, and I spent part of the day with Gaia, because she was devastated as well. Primo wasn't that well-known then, in England.

EM: In England and in the United States, because of course he was well-known in Italy.

PR: Oh yes. So that was . . . We had a wonderful meeting, and then . . .

EM: You know, my father also went to see him not long before that time and asked for a text of his about the Jewish cemetery in Venice. At that time my father, who was born in Venice, was the President of a Committee for the Jewish historical center of Venice; so he asked him for a preface to a volume on the ancient cemetery of the Jewish community of Venice. And Primo Levi wrote this preface. But the volume with this "Premessa" ("Premise"), written in November 1985, which appears in the first of the two volumes on the Jewish Cemetery of Venice (*La comunità ebraica di Venezia e il suo antico cimitero*, 2 vols., edited by Aldo Luzzatto, Milano: Il Polifilo 2000), was published only in 2000, when Primo Levi was no longer alive, and neither was my father. After that visit in Turin my father told me—I don't know if you had the same feeling when you went to Primo Levi's home—he told me he felt a somber atmosphere, with so many women of the family around who looked very aged, old.

PR: There was his old mother.

EM: There was his mother, there were other old people around, and he felt an atmosphere of somberness. I don't know if you did.

PR: Well, I knew that the mother was a tremendous burden for him, because she wouldn't let anybody else touch her but Primo: feed her, bedpan her . . . But Primo and I hit it off, we hit it off. And so we had lots of light-hearted conversations . . . What's the name of that essay about the Venice cemetery? We can see there, I have a big black and white book of Primo Levi's works there on the table, right on the table there, right there. That's a collection.

EM: This one? *The Complete Works of Primo Levi,* edited by Anne Goldstein and published in 2015. So then I will check inside.

PR: Check the name, I'll probably find it there.

BOOK JACKETS AND THE JEWISH CENTURY

EM: Yes, I will see if it's there. But now, could you tell me something about the covers of your books?

PR: Mostly I have used a wonderful designer, who is a friend, named Milton Glaser. He is a great graphic designer, and he designed many of the jackets, the late jackets.

EM: At the beginning, you started with that cover by your brother for your first book, *Goodbye, Columbus.* I don't know if you remember, when the short novel came out in *The Paris Review,* there was an illustration.

PR: Yes, I remember that one.

EM: It was about the black boy.

PR: Oh, is that right?

EM: Yes, it's a wonderful illustration.

PR: Yes, I don't know who did it . . . Let's turn some light on. Today is the shortest day of the year. Yes, December 21st.

EM: We are meeting on the shortest day of the year! . . . Oh, I see a book here, *The Jewish Century* by Yuri Slezkine.

PR: This is a fascinating book! I've just finished it. (*Handing it over.*) It's a brilliant book. He's brilliant, this fellow.

EM: Thank you. Oh, with Chagall on the cover . . . The titles of the chapters are great. "The Jews and Other Nomads," "Swann's Nose." . . .

PR: "Swann's Nose" is good, yes.

EM: "Babel's First Love," "The Jews and Three Promised Lands." Very interesting.

PR: Yes, Promised Lands were Soviet Russia, Palestine, and New York.

EM: That's wonderful, I see how you underline!

PR: Well, I was fascinated reading this book. He's quite brilliant, this guy. He teaches at the University of California, Berkeley. He has just written a new book, it's called *The House of Government*, about the Russian Revolution, about twelve families who had an apartment in a house, and what happened to each family during the Revolution and after. So I want to get hold of that. But this is wonderful.

EM: You know, this cover with Chagall reminds me of Benjamin Harshav, who wrote two wonderful books on Chagall and Yiddish culture. There was a panel on him at the conference of the Association for Jewish Studies in Washington a few days ago, where there was also a panel on my book *Writing for Justice*. I'm reminded of Harshav by this cover of *The Jewish Century*. So, talking about covers and illustrations, you probably have *The Paris Review* issue.

PR: Yes, I think I have it in the country.

EM: I may send you the illustration. Because it's a surprise, nobody thinks that character has been given such importance in the publication of the review. It suggests a new way of reading the story, without focusing on the two lovers, but on the boy. But I have noticed that, after that first cover by your brother, at a certain point you seem to prefer covers without illustrations.

PR: That is because I found the illustrations they selected so banal. But then I found photography, when years went by, and we did have photography on the cover. And then Milton Glaser and I were living in a town called Woodstock, up in New York, and Milton was living there. He did one cover, I think maybe *The Counterlife* was the first cover he did. And then he did practically all, right down till the end.

EM: What can you tell me about the big change you introduced in the year 2000, when at the beginning of your books, just before the title page, you began listing all your titles no longer chronologically but in groups of books? When and why did you start thinking that *that* was a new way of presenting your works?

PR: Was that in the year 2000?

EM: In the year 2000 for the first time, with *The Human Stain.*

PR: I think I wanted to draw readers' attention to the fact that some of these books belong together, they weren't just a long list of books. In fact, they began to see Zuckerman as a character because I had put all those books together. And Kepesh as a character, I think I'd written two or three of the Kepesh books by then. And then these Roth books. So it seemed to me a good idea. I think it's been effective actually, I think it focused people, inasmuch as you can focus them.

EM: You know, I'm very proud of the fact that in our *Meridiani Mondadori* edition, in the bibliography, I was able to have both lists, the chronological list of titles *and* this list of titles by groups.

PR: Oh good. Does that book have *all* the titles of *all* books?

EM: Yes. And I think that's something that is very important, because in the Italian Einaudi editions you wouldn't see the list of titles you started in the year 2000, but only a chronological list. So for the first time, and this is something that also *La Pléiade* does not have, I think, we have the lists of titles written in both ways, chronologically and by groups of books. Concerning your new collection *Why Write?*, I noticed that there you have kept all the interviews in the *Shop Talk* and not all of the texts in the other collection, *Reading Myself and Others.*

PR: Well, the writers I wrote about in *Reading Myself and Others* are obscurer. And I left out anything that was topical, too topical, into the sixties and seventies. And also, I didn't like some of them, you know. And also I redid some of those essays too, I mean I changed the wording in some of them. I didn't change the arguments. It's just editing. I wasn't such a good writer, you know.

EM: There is an interview with yourself that you did on *The Great American Novel.* I remember there was a sentence that I wanted to know more about, but you have omitted that text.

PR: Yes, because nobody has read that book!

EM: The first volume of the *Meridiani Mondadori* includes eight of your novels written between 1959 and 1986, arriving at *The Counterlife*. I personally find this novel extremely important from all points of view: for the debate, for the structure . . .

PR: It's a good book. Something shifted, my works changed. That's the kind of pivot on which you change, because I got the idea of complexity and amplification. And in the earlier novels, except for *Letting Go*, which was a young creation, but in the early ones I was very . . . condensing. And then with *The Counterlife* I opened up and allowed the complexity in. And it changed everything that came after, till the last. The last four books became rather simple again.

EM: With *The Counterlife* you explored the possibility of creating alternative stories, showing how reality can take different turns.

PR: As it does!

EM: Yes, as it does! Depending on our choices as well, but . . .

PR: . . . but sometimes not!

GOODBYE, COLUMBUS, PORTNOY'S COMPLAINT, *AND AN "ATLANTIC FIRST"*

EM: I finally have a few specific questions. One is about *Goodbye, Columbus*. I was wondering whether the title *Goodbye, Columbus*, in part referring to Columbus, Ohio, was also in honor of your editor Starbuck, who was born there: George Starbuck. You didn't know, maybe. He was born in Columbus, Ohio! Was the coincidence just by chance?

PR: He never told me! No, I thought it was something amusing about people standing on the shore, saying to Columbus who had discovered America, "Goodbye," "Goodbye, Columbus." You know, Christopher Columbus went on a great journey, and so does my young hero. *Goodbye, Columbus* comes from that song, the college song, but I imagined that it had to do with Columbus, Christopher Columbus.

EM: The song . . . ?

PR: There's a college where the brother goes. It isn't a song, it's someone narrating.

EM: Exactly. Yes, of course, there is that wonderful, very imperial voice, describing the end of college life and the beginning of a new life, so in a way it's saying good-bye to one's life as a young person and beginning the life as an adult. And, of course, at the same time it's creating a parallel with the American experience of arriving at a New World . . .

PR: Yes, of discovering America!

EM: When did you precisely start writing *Goodbye, Columbus*? I have seen different dates mentioned concerning when you started writing this text, which of course you began under the impulse of your friend Stern's advice. Did you start in 1957 or in 1958? In a letter to your editor Starbuck, which I was able to read in an essay by a scholar, you told him that you had just started writing it in March 1958. But somewhere else I read that you wrote it immediately after your friend's advice in 1957. Do you remember when you started really?

PR: Let me think. I started in '58, March '58?

EM: Well, that's what you wrote in your letter, maybe it was just a letter to an editor, saying: Oh look, I have a story that I have just started . . .

PR: If I started in March '58 and it was published in February '59, it was too soon. I probably started in '57.

EM: And then in 1958, when they insisted that they wanted a novel and not the short stories, you said: Oh, I have a story which I have just started. Instead you had it already, probably.

PR: That's right, probably.

EM: There is a question I have about *Portnoy's Complaint*. When you started publishing the first chapter in the magazine, did you already know that you were writing the whole novel?

PR: No. The first part appeared in *Esquire*. It was called "A Jewish Patient Begins His Analysis." And, no, I had no idea. And then I just thought: go on, just keep going. And I wrote it and published it, I had never done that before, or since. Wrote it and published it, and it began to get a lot of attention . . . I don't like the end of that book. It lacks the texture of the earlier stuff: the stuff about the family, the stuff about Newark, the stuff about sex, has texture. The last section in Israel is thin, it's very thin, and forced, I think. I didn't know enough, you know. I think I'd been, yes, I'd been to Israel in '62 for a month, but I was inventing a hollow place. I don't like the ending of that book.

EM: Maybe the whole chapter is a bit weak. But the conclusion, the last paragraphs are good. There is the explosion, Portnoy's voice, his "howl" . . .

PR: Right. But the scene with the Israeli soldier is not good.

EM: Anyhow the novel grew little by little, by publishing it in magazines. In a way, like nineteenth-century writers, like Dickens, who were publishing by installments, while writing.

PR: Yes, I'd never done that before or since.

EM: But publishing in magazines a book that would come out as a novel in book form is something that you have done very frequently.

PR: Yes, but I am not alone in that. It's done by many American writers. I think I have published in *The Atlantic,* and in *The New Yorker,* and in *The New American Review.* That was a wonderful magazine.

EM: Yes, it was wonderful. Its format . . .

PR: It was the '60s. The sixties were just so full of life and audacity, you know.

EM: By the way, since you mentioned *The Atlantic.* I remember that at a certain point in your novel *The Anatomy Lesson* Zuckerman is proud of having published a story in *The Atlantic* as a young man, an "Atlantic First." I think that was a column.

PR: That's right, it used to be. *The Atlantic* used to pick an unknown writer and publish it, I think you got paid a little more, it was called an "Atlantic First."

EM: So that's what you meant by saying "an 'Atlantic First,'" referring to the fact of having published there.

PR: Yes! You know these books too well!

***

It is moving for me who was there to listen again to Roth's voice, enjoying the marvel of the almost three hours I spent with him in intense, exciting conversation. I hope the transcript of the central part of this meeting conveys something of that experience—the wealth of information, the insights about his life, and his perceptions about his work—though what is lost in a transcript is the soft, suave tone of his voice, the frequent moments of laughter that punctuated our talk, and his relaxed physical presence, while sitting in his leather chair, or standing to take a photo from the wall or a book from a stack on the table. Nor can I, for lack of space, report here all the other recollections I have of our conversation, which actually continued on other matters of common interest on that long, memorable winter afternoon. Not many days after our meeting, the *New York Times* of January 16, 2018, published an interview with him by Charles McGrath, which had actually taken place, as specified at the start of the article, a few weeks before our meeting. In a passage of that interview there is a remark Roth made on the *Meridiani Mondadori* volume I edited, which conveys his "humbling sense of wonder and satisfaction" with the publication of that volume (the episode is also reported in the Fall 2018 issue of *The Philip Roth Society Newsletter*, from which the previously quoted words are taken):

> *"Just look at this," he said to me last month, holding up the ornately bound Mondadori volume, as thick as a Bible and comprising titles like "Lamento di Portnoy" and "Zuckerman Scatenato." "Who reads books like this?"*

I had a copy of that volume with me when we met that December day, and he inscribed his dedication on it, written in strong black characters, which reads: "*To Elèna Mortara, in gratitude for this splendid volume, Philip Roth, 2017*": a wonderful, generous gift to me, and one more testimony of his appreciation and satisfaction. I am relieved when I think that he was able to see his entrance into the major literary cathedrals, or temples, of Italian and French book culture, and that he seemed to enjoy that literary recognition coming from across the ocean.

At the end of that day, sometime after sunset, while I was leaving, Roth showed me the satirical drawings hanging next to the front door at the entrance of his apartment. They were the famous drawings by Philip Guston inspired by his novel *The Breast*: his grotesquely self-ironical version of Kafka's novella *The Metamorphosis*, telling of professor David Kepesh, who, obsessed by sex, finds himself "inexplicably" transformed into a gigantic breast. With a tone between seriousness and playfulness he remarked, with some pride: "With this novel, I anticipated the transgender culture!" He knew he had been revolutionary and not always understood. Upon my leaving, we hugged each other, next to the door. In parting from him—he who still looked so tall and straight and was so kindly warm to me—I thought that ours was a friendly and promising goodbye, *un arrivederci*, as we say in Italian; instead, it was a final adieu, *un addio*.

WORKS CITED

Bassani, Giorgio. *The Garden of the Finzi-Continis*, translated by Isabel Quigly, Atheneum, 1965.

Bellow, Saul. *The Victim*. Vanguard Press, 1947.

Bulgheroni, Marisa. *Il nuovo romanzo americano 1945-1959*. Schwarz, 1960.

---. "Philip Roth, ritratto del giovane scrittore. New York, 1959-Milano, 2011." *Chiamatemi Ismaele. Racconto della mia America*. il Saggiatore, 2013, pp. 83-86.

Harshav, Benjamin. *Marc Chagall and His Times. A Documentary Narrative*, translated from Russian, Yiddish, French, German, and Hebrew by Benjamin and Barbara Harshav, Stanford UP, 2003.

---, editor. *Marc Chagall on Art and Culture*. Stanford UP, 2003.

Kafka, Franz. "The Metamorphosis." *The Great Wall of China. Stories and Reflections*, translated by Willa and Edwin Muir, Martin Secker, 1933.

Levi, Primo. "Premessa" (November 1985). *La Comunità ebraica di Venezia e il suo antico cimitero*, edited by Aldo Luzzatto, introduction by Alberto Mortara, vol. I, Il Polifilo, 2000, pp. xiii-xv.

---. *The Complete Works of Primo Levi*, edited by Anne Goldstein, introduction by Toni Morrison, vols. I, II, III, Liveright, 2015.

Mauro, Walter, and Elena Clementelli, editors. "Philip Roth." *La trappola e la nudità. Lo scrittore e il potere*. Rizzoli, 1974, pp. 254-65.

McGrath, Charles. "No Longer Writing, Philip Roth Still Has Plenty to Say" (Interview). *The New York Times*, 16 January 2018.

Mortara, Elèna. *Writing for Justice: Victor Séjour, the Kidnapping of Edgardo Mortara, and the Age of Transatlantic Emancipations*. Dartmouth College P, 2015.

Nadel, Ira. "Roth @ 25: Publishing *Goodbye, Columbus*." *Roth after Eighty: Philip Roth and the American Literary Imagination*, edited by David Gooblar and Aimee Pozorski, Lexington, 2017, pp. 19-27.

Roth, Philip. *American Pastoral*. Houghton Mifflin, 1997.

---. *The Anatomy Lesson*. Farrar, Straus and Giroux, 1983.

---. *The Breast*. Holt, Rinehart and Winston, 1972.

---. *The Counterlife*. Farrar, Straus and Giroux, 1986.

---. "Eric Duncan." *Why Write?*, pp. 346-48.

---. *The Ghost Writer*. Farrar, Straus and Giroux, 1979.

---. "Goodbye, Columbus." *The Paris Review*, No. 20, Autumn-Winter 1958-59, pp. 70-179.

---. *Goodbye, Columbus and Five Short Stories*. Houghton Mifflin, 1959.

---. *The Great American Novel*. Holt, Rinehart and Winston, 1973.

---. *The Human Stain*. Houghton Mifflin, 2000.

---. "'I Always Wanted You to Admire My Fasting'; or, Looking at Kafka." *Why Write?*, pp. 5-24.

---. "A Jewish Patient Begins His Analysis." *Esquire*, April 1967, pp. 104, 107, 191-93.

---. *Lamento di Portnoy*. In *Romanzi. Volume primo, 1959-1986*, translated by Roberto C. Sonaglia, pp. 131-363.

---. *Letting Go*. Random House, 1962.

---. *My Life as a Man*. Holt, Rinehart and Winston, 1974.

---. "On *The Great American Novel*." *Reading Myself and Others*, pp. 75-92.

---. *Operation Shylock: A Confession*. Simon and Schuster, 1993.

---. *Philip Roth: The Library of America Edition*. 9 vols, chronology and notes by Ross Miller, The Library of America, 2005-2013.

---. *The Plot Against America*. Houghton Mifflin, 2004.

---. *Portnoy's Complaint*. Random House, 1969.

---. *The Prague Orgy.* 1985. Vintage, 1996.

---. *The Professor of Desire.* Farrar, Straus and Giroux, 1977.

---. *Reading Myself and Others.* Farrar, Straus and Giroux, 1975.

---. *Romans et nouvelles 1959-1977,* edited by Brigitte Félix, Aurélie Guillain, Paule Lévy, and Ada Savin, preface by Philippe Jaworski, Gallimard, Bibliothèque de La Pléiade, 2017.

---. *Romanzi. Volume primo, 1959-1986,* edited and with an introduction by Elèna Mortara, Meridiani Mondadori, 2017.

---. *Shop Talk: A Writer and His Colleagues and Their Work.* Houghton, 2001.

---. "Some New Jewish Stereotypes." *Reading Myself and Others,* pp. 137-47.

---. *Why Write? Collected Nonfiction 1960-2013.* The Library of America, 2017.

---. "Writing and the Powers That Be." *Reading Myself and Others,* pp. 3-13.

"Roth's Work Published in *Meridiani Mondadori.*" *The Philip Roth Society Newsletter,* vol. 12, no. 2, Fall 2018, p. 10.

Slezkine, Yuri. *The House of Government. A Saga of the Russian Revolution.* Princeton UP, 2017.

---. *The Jewish Century.* 2004. Princeton UP, 2006.

ARTICLE

Reading Roth/
Reading Ourselves
Looking Back

Victoria Aarons

In "The Ruthless Intimacy of Fiction," an address delivered by Roth on the occasion of his eightieth birthday celebration at the Newark Museum in 2013 and published in the recent Library of America collection of his nonfiction (2017), Roth argues that at the "heart" of the realist novel is the "passion for specificity," the attentiveness to the particularity of experience, to "the hypnotic materiality of the world one is in" (393). The attention to detail, to the seemingly trivial mundanities and minutiae that make up a life—the flotsam left in one's wake—is the stuff and substance of the novelist's craft. But it is also the material landscape to which we, as readers of fiction, are drawn, the "hypnotic" allure, the fixation on those things that ground us in this life, that root us in the commonality but at the same time the uniqueness of our experience. The quotidian thus takes on deep emotional resonance for Roth. The task, then, of the novelist is to "rummage around in memory" for the myriad of observable details to enact life on the page ("Ruthless Intimacy" 392-93). It is the artful representation of the familiar, of the real, in all its "concreteness," its specificity and particularity, that seems to recreate for Roth the heady experience of being alive. As Roth puts it, "without the crucial representation of what is real, there is nothing [. . . .] It is from a scrupulous fidelity to the blizzard of specific data [. . .] from the force of its uncompromising attentiveness, from its *physicalness*, that the realistic novel, the insatiable realistic novel with its multitude of realities, derives its ruthless intimacy. And its mission: to portray humanity in its particularity" ("Ruthless Intimacy" 393; italics in original). This "ruthless intimacy" at the center of Roth's fiction, including the stark materiality of complex human motive, derives its uncompromising realism from those pinpoints of targeted vulnerability, the sharp arrows directed to those most uncomfortable places of evasion and prevarication: ruthless because relentless, the novelist's undistracted eye focused on the host of maneuverings and disarrangements that make up a life; intimate because of its piercing clarity and familiarity—"No hocus-pocus," as the narrator of *Everyman* regretfully admits (51). No amount of strategic plotting, of self-reinvention, and of the attempts to escape history—the unanticipated ambushes of history and the history of one's own making—can safeguard Roth's characters from the betrayals of self and others. The juxtapositions of the material and the existential, then, create the conditions for Roth's realism, a realism based in large part on the playful anatomy of the invented, reimagined self, participating in the fantasy of, as Nathan Zuckerman puts it, "turning what-was into what-wasn't or what-might-be into what-was" (*The Counterlife* 38), or, as the protagonist of *Indignation* longingly wishes, "if only this and if only that" (229).

Roth thus presents his characters as figures bearing the very seductive possibility of a "multitude of realities." Disenchanted with a worn-out, dampened, banal, and diminished life, one can slip into another, "an exchange of existences," as the wily Zuckerman says. But, in changing those distasteful and objectionable aspects of one's existence, one would do well to caution against the intemperate, impulsive desire, the head-long rush to "change *everything*," as Zuckerman chastises his brother Henry (*Counterlife* 156; italics in original). In other words, one would do well to show some restraint, as Roth's characters more often than not humorously fail to do, only too late recognizing, as does the narrator of *Indignation*, that even "the tiniest, littlest things do have tragic consequences" (14). One cannot, finally, walk out of one life into another without fallout, without, that is, the inevitable repercussions for the treachery and betrayals teeming around individual action. For Roth, however, the trick, the sleight-of-hand, is the agility of pretense, to "pretend to be anything we want. All it takes is impersonation," which as Zuckerman promises, "is like saying that it takes only courage" (*Counterlife* 367). Roth's characters often struggle with questions of what knowledge to retain and what to discard. Roth describes his own trajectory from the provincialism and insularity of his upbringing to the expanded worlds opening to the young novelist in terms of such dualities: as a matter of navigating and arbitrating "the desire to repudiate and the desire to cling, a sense of allegiance and the need to rebel, the alluring dream of escaping into the challenging unknown and the counter-dream of holding fast to the familiar" (Preface xiii-xiv). The reader of Roth's fiction is thus carried along by the allure of the intoxicating performance of strategic self-impersonation, by the drama of self-transformation, and by the possibility of stepping out of one existence—the one messily bequeathed to us—and into another redemptive and paradisiacal one, the elaborate if stumbling creation of "imagined worlds, often green and breastlike, where we may finally be 'ourselves'" (*Counterlife* 369). Of course, as Roth ironically reminds us, we all know what happened in that mythological paradise when we tried to be "ourselves." Such transgressive delights have never been, in the Solomonic words of another Rothian character, particularly "good-for-the-Jews" ("The Conversion of the Jews" 150).

Reading Roth has always been, and continues to be, an invitation to the kind of "ruthless intimacy" that turns the critical gaze back toward the reader. If we are honest brokers about our participation in, as Zuckerman would have it, the ventriloquy of self-impersonation, in reading Roth we come to see ourselves and the contingencies of our situation in all their "particularity," the plenitude and want of both our self-made and externally imposed worlds, "the kind of stories that people turn life into, the kind of lives that people turn stories into" (*Counterlife* 111). We come to see the performative aspects of our maneuverings—those "strategies of aggression [. . .] strategies of retreat," as Nathan Marx in "Defender of the Faith" puts it (194)—mirrored, as Roth says in a 2016 interview with Daniel Sandstrom, in "the plight he has invented for his characters [. . .] the lifelike ramifications of the ensemble they make" ("Interview *Svenska Dagbladet*" 387). For the honest reader of Roth's fiction, there is no turning from the direct gaze that confronts us; there is nowhere to run, caught off guard by the treachery of human impulses and desire and "ambushed [. . .] by the unpredictability that is history" ("My Uchronia" 345). In other words, in reading Roth well, that is, reading Roth un-blinkered, the reader is confronted with the great finality that accosts the narrator of *Everyman*, that "There's no remaking reality" (5), or, as Arnie Mesnikoff, the narrator of *Nemesis*, reminds us, "the tyranny of contingency—is everything" (243). Thus, in exposing the mundanities, the absurdities, the strategic choreographies, and the exigencies of our experience, Roth taught us to read ourselves.

In this way, and in others, after over half a century of prolific and distinguished literary productivity, Roth remains a primary, even primal, voice of American cultural, intellectual, and literary conscience. And Roth's America, in all its particularities and peculiarities, is a landscape with which we are—if not entirely, comfortably at home—then keenly familiar. As is, of course, Roth. To the very core, Roth is an American writer, writing, as he says, in "the American moment" ("I Have Fallen in Love with American Names" 47). As Roth suggests, for the native-born writer of his generation, as tangled up as his writing was with Jewish identity and history (especially during the repositioning of the post-war period), "The American adventure was one's engulfing fate [. . . .] As a novelist, I think of myself and have from the beginning, as [. . .] irrefutably American [. . .] under the spell of the country's past, partaking of its drama and destiny" ("I Have Fallen in Love with American Names" 47). Roth is an American Jewish writer of his time and place, enveloped by that history, growing up at a time when "the definition of the Jew" took on "such stunning emotional and historical proportions" ("Interview with *Le Nouvel Observateur*"131). In an essentializing, formative way, Roth's agitating company of characters become metonymic reflections of Roth's restless, mutating America. His characters' limitations represent America's limitations, the landscape that has shaped them, just as they, from the materiality of its spiraling center—"every last American thing"—have been shaped ("Ruthless Intimacy" 393). "America," then, is part of the ensemble of recurring Rothian characters; their fates are entwined. America is seared behind the lenses of his characters' visions of themselves, their making, their stories, and their place in history. Roth's characters, as well as the playground of his fictional landscape, America, find themselves in a similarly untenable situation, both on shaky grounds with stories that need defending, in a demanding ethical register of "character." The "everyman" of Roth's thus named novel concedes: "No one could say there wasn't enough sadness to go around or enough remorse to prompt the fugue of questions with which he attempted to defend the story of his life" (95). Such a regretful afterthought might well be attributed to America itself. The making of character, for Roth, thus extends to the comportment and disposition of an age. Both America and the protagonists of the country's drama-in-the-making are on the novelist's couch. America is the "patient," just as Roth's characters—and by extension his readers—are. And both might be said to be characterized by their limitations, their missteps, and miscalculations, in other words, by what they are not but might have been. Thus, the character of Roth's America, like *Everyman's* protagonist, might well be thought of as defined, thwarted, saddened, and "assailed by remorse not just for this mistake but for all his mistakes, all the ineradicable, stupid, inescapable mistakes—swept away by the misery of his limitations" (158).

And who knows this better than Roth? After all, as he famously analogized in a 1981 interview with French essayist Alain Finkielkraut for *Le Nouvel Observateur*, "America is the place I know best in the world. It's the only place I know in the world. My consciousness and my language were shaped by America. I'm an American writer in ways that a plumber isn't an American plumber or a miner an American miner or a cardiologist an American cardiologist. Rather, what the heart is to the cardiologist, the coal to the miner, the kitchen sink to the plumber, America is to me" ("Interview with *Le Nouvel Observateur*"133-34). That is, America is the artifact, the substance that Roth shapes and excavates for possible punctures and wounds, the center stage for the imagination. In other words, America is the defining and motivating point of origin and source of knowledge for Roth's fiction. His body of fiction is tangled up in the ever-mutating "American moment." As Roth has suggested all along, America is tough competition for the novelist's imagination. In "Writing American Fiction," Roth argues that "the American writer [. . .] has his hands full in trying to understand, describe, and then make *credible* much of American reality. It stupefies, it sickens, it infuriates, and finally it is even a kind of embarrassment to one's one meager imagination. The actuality is continually outdoing our talents, and the culture tosses up figures almost daily that are the envy of any novelist" ("Writing American Fiction," 176; italics in original). There is a kind of absurd implausibility for Roth in America's persistent condition of self-reinvention, symptomatic of the unguarded, unmeasured, frantic attempts, not unlike those of Roth's characters, to defend its own stories. This fraught condition is no doubt even truer now, in the opening decades of the twenty-first century, than it was in 1960 when Roth first wrote this piece.

Roth has written that "The treacherous imagination is everybody's maker—we are all the invention of each other, everybody a conjuration conjuring up everyone else. We are all each other's authors" (*Counterlife* 164). But we are all each other's readers as well. Roth's attention to ironic detail in his fiction is not only theorized in his prose but is also a characteristic of that prose. Roth, in telling us how to read him, also embodies the concerns of how he thinks he should be read. As Roth has said, "At best writers change the *way* readers read" ("Interview with *The Paris Review*" 170; italics in original). For the better part of the past century, Roth has posed for readers a view of America and of themselves that is unrelenting in its honesty and perspicacity. In changing the *way* we read, Roth has changed the ways in which we view the worlds in which we live. In doing so, Roth forces both the backward glance and the inward gaze. Like Neil Klugman, one is compelled to see his or her "reflection," to have "looked [. . .] in the mirror," and, as Roth's prototype uncomfortably but not entirely unwelcomingly manages to do, "looked hard at the image of me, at that darkening of the glass, and then my gaze pushed through it" ("Goodbye, Columbus" 136). Roth is, after all, a realist, and realism requires the energy and the courage to look frankly at one's character and one's place in history, to look head-on and without blinders, but also with humor, with farcical, skeptical, self-parodic, self-ironic, and self-critical recognition, but with humor nonetheless. Thus said, reading Roth is and always has been, as even the deeply suspicious Yakov Blotnik would admit, "good-for-the-Jews" ("Conversion" 150). Roth, the deeply self-proclaimed American writer, is too, in the end, a deeply American Jewish writer, a historically important voice in the production of American Jewish identity in the past half century.

WORKS CITED

Roth, Philip. "The Conversion of the Jews." *Goodbye Columbus and Five Short Stories*. Houghton,1989, pp. 139-58.

---. *The Counterlife*. Farrar, 1986.

---. "Defender of the Faith." *Goodbye Columbus and Five Short Stories*. Houghton, 1989, pp. 161-200.

---. *Everyman*. Houghton, 2006.

---. "I Have Fallen in Love with American Names." *The New Yorker*, June 5 & 12, 2017, pp. 46-47.

---. *Indignation*. Houghton, 2008.

---. "Interview with *Le Nouvel Observateur*." *Why Write? Collected Nonfiction 1960-2013*. Library of America, 2017, pp. 123-34.

---. "Interview with *Svenska Dagbladet*." *Why Write? Collected Nonfiction 1960-2013*. Library of America, 2017, pp. 379-87.

---. "My Uchronia." *Why Write? Collected Nonfiction 1960-2013*. Library of America, 2017, pp. 336-45.

---. *Nemesis*. Houghton, 2010.

---. "Preface to the Thirtieth Anniversary Edition." *Goodbye Columbus and Five Short Stories*. Houghton, 1989.

---. "The Ruthless Intimacy of Fiction." *Why Write? Collected Nonfiction 1960-2013*. Library of America, 2017, pp. 391-404.

---. "Writing American Fiction." Reading Myself and Others. Penguin, 1985, pp. 173-191.

ARTICLE

Remembering Roth

The Sharp Mustard Flavor
of *The Human Stain*

Ann Basu

Philip Roth intrigued, provoked, amused, and absorbed his readers for more than fifty years. Challenging and delighting us, his novels have generated an intellectual response from writers and scholars that has created one of the most vibrant literary fields in modern literary criticism. Roth declared that he would write no more fiction after *Nemesis*, published in 2010. Now he is gone, and we can only await his official biography written by Blake Bailey and continue to speak amongst ourselves about his great literary legacy.

Roth was an American to his core. His Jewish family and upbringing shaped his vision of a nation whose culture he never stopped exploring and whose flaws he dissected in ever more powerful ways. The nature of Roth's contribution to his national culture is perhaps best expressed in Roth's conversation with Primo Levi in 1986, when Roth asks Levi to explain "the tension between your rootedness and your impurity" as a Jew and an Italian. Levi returns:

> I see no contradiction between "rootedness" and being (or feeling) "a grain of mustard." To feel oneself a catalyst, a spur to one's cultural environment [. . .] it is an advantage to belong to a (not necessarily racial) minority [. . .] don't you feel yourself, you, Philip Roth, "rooted" in your country and at the same time "a mustard grain"? In your books I perceive a sharp mustard flavor (*Shop* 13).

There is much truth in Levi's observation. Roth's novels are sharp and pungent granules within American culture at the same time as being thoroughly within the grain of that culture; they are incisive, provocative, and sometimes outrageous. His scrutiny of his country and its culture will be desperately missed.

My love for Roth's fiction began with *The Human Stain* (2000), the third novel of his American trilogy published after *American Pastoral* (1997) and *I Married a Communist* (1998). Before this novel cropped up on my English

Literature masters reading list, the only contact I had had with Roth's work was his first short story collection, *Goodbye Columbus,* and his notorious *Portnoy's Complaint* that I didn't know how to make sense of in the lurid light of its celebrity. I was little-prepared for the mature, sweeping, masterly accomplishment that was *The Human Stain.* I became immersed in the story of the racially-passing Coleman Silk and of Coleman Silk's America, to a depth that I have rarely experienced.

The fascination with *The Human Stain* that drew me to Roth's work began with the shock of finding out that its "Jewish" and "white" protagonist, Coleman Silk, was a light-skinned black man who, in his youth, had made a fateful decision to pass as white, using Jewishness as a cover identity to explain features like his curly hair. Crucially, Roth hides the fundamental fact about Coleman's "passing" for the novel's first eighty-five pages. The revelation about Coleman's race highlights the truth that when we read we complete the meanings of the text from our own imaginations—an activity that Roth continually problematizes. His work, to a greater degree than many writers', induces an imbalance or oscillation in readers' minds as we establish predictive patterns from the text but are nevertheless made jarringly aware of other temporarily excluded meanings, like Coleman's "alien" blackness. We are thus continually brought to test our own judgments about Roth's novels.

My own reaction to Coleman's blackness startled me. I was disoriented by the revelation. The knowledge of Coleman's secret brought me right up against my preconceptions about the character, reconfiguring my category of "what-is-Coleman." I was knocked off-balance, compelled to revisit scenes from the book in the light of my new knowledge. This act of re-reading also made me reflect long, deeply, and uncomfortably on my understanding of race and racial categories. Philip Roth challenged me to do some real work on his text and on myself and hooked me on his writing.

The Human Stain's exploration of American identity under pressure boils down to the word "spooks." Coleman, an established and successful academic at Athena College, ill-advisedly uses "spooks" to describe two absentee black students on his class register whom he has never seen. Overlooking the word's covert meaning as a racist term for a black person, he argues that "spooks" is intended to mean "ghostly." Nevertheless, that fateful word initiates a complaint of racial harassment by the absent students who have understood "spooks" to be a racial slur and triggers college disciplinary hearings that bring about Coleman's resignation and withdrawal from public life. On the rebound from this disaster he becomes scandalously, and ultimately fatally, involved with Faunia Farley, Athena's young white female janitor.

The Human Stain questions the authority of the word itself, while demonstrating Roth's powerful and rigorous command of words and their history. It is set in the 1990s at the time of President Bill Clinton's impeachment for perjury following Clinton's sexual misconduct with Monica Lewinsky and his declaration that will haunt him, "I did not have sexual relations with that woman." An era of "speech wars" forms the backdrop to both Coleman Silk's harassment charges and the Clinton impeachment, resembling each other in being trials by public opinion as much as legal processes. Roth shows how the puritanical strand in American culture underpins much of the debate about these occurrences, criticizing puritanism for its rigidly categorical approach to human sexual activity that leads to a hypocritical moralism acting as a cover for racism and anti-Semitism. By focusing on the loaded term "spooks," *The Human Stain* pulls together legal, political, public, and literary debates around race and sex that are highly contemporary to the 1990s but also imbue the history of America's racial and sexual politics. In the light of the #MeToo movement, Trump's America, and the Kavanaugh confirmation process these debates have gone through yet another convolution to which we can but imagine Roth's response.

Roth was always highly conscious of the literary legacy upon which he drew. *The Human Stain*'s take on race is given much of its literary context by Ralph Ellison's *Invisible Man* (1952), from which comes the race-based word bomb, "lily-white," that echoes in Roth's novel. "Lily-white" comes "flying from [Coleman's] mouth" when Coleman visits his lawyer, Nelson Primus, after being anonymously threatened with exposure of his affair with Faunia and harassed by Faunia's violent ex-husband (*Stain* 84). Primus castigates Coleman for the affair, whereupon Coleman swears that he never again wants to see Primus's "smug fucking lily-white face" (*Stain* 81). Coleman's outburst astonishes both Primus and Coleman himself. Primus remains unaware of the racial charge of "lily-white," while we are just about to discover Coleman's hidden black identity. Through this descriptor Roth aligns the scene with *Invisible Man*'s scene where Ellison's black protagonist reveals his self-humiliation at pleasing white people and attracting praise from the "most lily-white men of the town" (18). Therefore, Coleman's furious epithet "lily-white" is more than a rejection of Primus's sanctimony; it is a repudiation of the lawyer's whiteness and a revelation of his own secret blackness. Like "spooks," "lily-white" is a key to the story of Coleman Silk by which Roth pays homage to *Invisible Man*, making the word inhabit *The Human Stain* to speak about race in America fifty years after Ellison.

Reading *The Human Stain* I began to see that Roth views his central characters as defendants, caught up in situations where both their personal and national identities are on trial. He reworks the "innocent" American of national mythology as a troubled and guilty individual who deceives himself and others and has a tormented relationship with his country. Robert Ferguson calls defendants "threshold people" in the court, occupying a liminal position in regard to identity: he says, "innocent until proven guilty but on the cusp, defendants can never remain where they are" (57). And Roth sees American-Jewish men in particular being perpetually on trial as Americans. Twentieth-century Jews, until at least the 1960s, were closely scrutinized and regarded with suspicion by more established Americans; they were given an in-between or liminal status as "trial members of the social compact" (Roediger 84). As Roth shows Coleman discovering, being Jewish is a fluid, liminal identity. It is always being tested by historical circumstance, vacillating between being perceived as American and un-American. This in-betweenness, with its continual movement between one state of being and another, tests the unity of both personal and national identity.

Coleman's story led me to the preceding books in Roth's American trilogy, where he had already powerfully woven together post-war American history and male identity. In *American Pastoral*, Seymour "the Swede" Levov is a kind of Jewish scout in the eyes of the narrator, Nathan Zuckerman: the Swede is "the boy we were all going to follow into America" in the 1950s (*Pastoral* 89). Although the young Swede appears to be a model of American manhood, a triumphant product of decades of integration, he finds himself at the center of a devastating generational and cultural conflict in the roiling, violent Vietnam era during which his daughter, Merry, becomes a fugitive bomber. The aftermath of her fatal act of violence all but destroys the Swede psychologically as his country implodes politically. In charting the depths of the Swede's desperation and disintegration Roth exposes the fractured, rapidly changing contours of American identity. In *I Married a Communist*, the secretive Ira Ringold, a national idol who voices Abraham Lincoln to enthusiastic public acclaim and has crafted a radio persona of the American common man, Iron Rinn, is revealed to be merely a performer—a fake American who has lied about his beliefs and aims. Ira, Zuckerman's adored mentor, is outed as a Communist and caught up in the McCarthy hearings intended to root out reds from American life. In rendering Ira's downfall through his trials in public hearings and in the media, Roth questions not only Ira's process of self-making but that of Zuckerman, whose self-formation is disrupted by Ira's deceptions and betrayals and who himself betrays Ira as his intense involvement with the man is followed by disillusionment. Exploring mid-twentieth-century American manhood and national identity during the decade of betrayal that was McCarthyism, Roth expands on the importance of the trial to self-making in America, continuing his project of probing and dismantling cultural narratives about the nation's unity, purity, and innocence.

Of all the American trilogy, *The Human Stain* is perhaps Roth's most persuasive rendition of a protagonist undergoing trials in the sense of physical ordeals, where the body is threatened with disintegration or contamination. Coleman Silk is a man in his seventies, past his physical and sexual peak like his friend and narrator, Zuckerman, and made more vulnerable by the emotional distress and anger caused by the harassment case. From early in Roth's career his novels have dealt with bodily ordeals, as with his farcical take on a Kafkaesque protagonist who becomes a human breast in *The Breast* (1973). In the American trilogy and other later novels, from *Operation Shylock* to *Nemesis*, Roth associates these bodily trials with tests of national identity generated by historical and political processes. The body of the individual who is at the center of the narrative then becomes important for its resemblance or lack of resemblance to the figurative body of the American nation. Strength, firmness, and well-boundedness, as well as whiteness and masculinity, are essential components of this American national body. The Jewish body, on the other hand, has been perceived as threateningly fluid, with Jews often seen as being alien to the national corpus, even as diseased—feared as a source of contamination. The boundaries of the American national body have changed over time but have also often been shored up by marginalizing Jews and women, as well as excluding black and other minorities. In exploring these processes of absorption and expulsion *The Human Stain* engages deeply with racial identity and racial politics in America. The racially ambiguous "half-visible" body of *The Human Stain's* Coleman Silk, a black man passing as white and Jewish, presents the American nation with an internal challenge based on racial division and turbulent and messy racial politics (*Stain* 213). Roth's ambiguous, performative Jewish selfhood is a manifestation of American selfhood that reveals its loosely bounded nature; in other words, there is no sense of the normal when Roth speaks of American identity in general.

I have felt shock and even disgust on occasions in response to Roth's novels, just as feelings of anger, guilt, shame, and disgust continually erupt from the characters themselves when they are called to account for the unacknowledged contradictions inherent in their self-making. Roth crafts moments that seem about to slip beyond even his control, as his protagonists reach their breaking point. One such eruption is the instant in *American Pastoral* at which the Swede's father, Lou Levov, has a fork jabbed into his face by a drunken dinner-guest—the same instant at which Lou and the Swede both understand that the post-war New World, in which they have implicitly believed, has foundered under the political impact of the Watergate crisis and the Nixon impeachment. Many scenes release strong feelings, often leavened by laughter that acts as a release valve when tensions get dangerously high. *Operation Shylock,* for instance, frequently strikes a note of frantic comedy, as when two maniacally-competing Philip Roths meet in an hotel: Philip Roth the writer-protagonist and Philip's namesake and nemesis whom he calls Moishe Pipik. The hotel scene ends by Moishe Pipik's exposing his unruly penis, stiffened by a prosthetic implant, in a final, crazed attempt to "prove" that he, too, is Philip Roth.

The Human Stain, like the whole of the American trilogy and Roth's other great novels such as *Operation Shylock, The Plot Against America,* and Roth's last novel, *Nemesis,* exposes the conflict at the heart of American self-making. It tests the mythology of national unity and revival: the ideological response to fears of national disintegration. It compellingly portrays the American Dream's unravelling during the decades between the end of the Second World War and the new millennium. In each of these major works, Roth strips the nation of its innocence and reinstates accountability at the heart of individual and national self-making.

My search for Roth's vision of America and American manhood led me to explore his body of work over ten years of completing a PhD and publishing a book, *States of Trial: Post-war American Manhood in Philip Roth's Later Novels* (2014). It was an exciting, frustrating, infuriating, fruitful period in which I grappled with works of awe-inspiring breadth and ambition, spacious novels about flawed individuals in demanding times, bursting with ideas about personal identity and nationality to be explored, appreciated and criticized. Philip Roth opened a path for me by which to understand America's history and sense of identity, while creating characters and scenes that will always live with me. For this I will always thank, honor, and miss him.

WORKS CITED

Ellison, Ralph. *Invisible Man.* Penguin, 1965.

Ferguson, Robert. *Trial in American Life.* U of Chicago P, 2007.

Roediger, David R. *Working Towards Whiteness: How America's Immigrants Became White; the Strange Journey from Ellis Island to the Suburbs.* Basic Books, 2005.

Roth, Philip. *American Pastoral.* Houghton, 1997.

---. *The Human Stain.* Houghton, 2000.

---. *Shop Talk.* Houghton, 2001.

ARTICLE

My Own Private Philip Roth

David Brauner

I heard the news of Philip Roth's death at 8:10 a.m. UK time on Wednesday 23rd May. I had just turned on BBC Radio 4 to listen to the "Today" news program, as is my custom on a working day, and I heard a voice I inferred was Blake Bailey's talking about Roth's work. I knew instantly that he must have passed away. I spent the next fifteen minutes or so listening to further tributes. In spite of Roth's eminence, I was surprised at the detailed coverage they were giving his death—it was the lead story for most of the morning on all BBC channels—and I was wondering if I would be asked to comment. At 9:00 a.m. I got a call from the people at the University of Reading press office asking me if I would be available for interviews with the media. They had already received inquiries from news channels in France, Germany, and Switzerland. When I got to the media suite on campus, there was a palpable buzz of excitement with which I felt ghoulishly complicit; the fact that Roth's death was also something of a career opportunity for his critics, I consoled myself by thinking, was an irony that he himself—always a ruthless opportunist when it came to mining the material offered by life for his career—would have appreciated. Nonetheless, I found the next few hours exhausting and stressful: while still trying to process the news of Roth's death I was having to summarize his achievements in brief soundbites for five-minute reports on media outlets. For the most part, I was asked the predictable questions: "Was he a misogynist?" (short answer, no; longer answer, he represented male sexuality, which can include elements of misogyny, unsparingly); "Why did he never win the Nobel?" (his work is too provocative and polarizing for the taste of the Swedish academy, who like to be able to issue cozy platitudes about the winning author); "What made him such an important writer?" (his restless reinvention of himself as a novelist, the power and intelligence of his writing). At the end of it all, I felt drained and somewhat cheapened and of course I felt that I had not done Roth justice.

The next day, at work, colleagues kept coming up to me in the corridor or knocking at my office door to offer their condolences. I thanked them but said that really it didn't feel particularly like a personal bereavement, because (a) I'd already mourned when Roth announced his retirement, while at the same time suspecting—hoping—that one final, posthumous work (*Notes For My Biographer?*) might appear, (b) he'd had a magnificent life, in which he'd achieved pretty much everything a writer could hope to achieve (the pesky absence of the Nobel notwithstanding) and (c) I didn't know the man personally. But in the days and weeks that followed I did begin, more and more, to feel Roth's death as a personal loss. Why? Partly because I've spent so many years reading, re-reading, teaching, and writing about him; but also because, however irrationally and unconsciously, I have come to feel that, at some level, I do enjoy a personal relationship with Roth; even that I own a part of him, my own private Philip Roth.

Certainly, I owe a lot to Roth, in professional terms. When I began writing about him, as a graduate student working on a PhD at University College London in the early 1990s, I felt that I was flying in the face of literary fashion. A number of senior academics warned me that Jewish-American literature had had its moment and that Roth in particular was old news, a spent force. The smart money in the literary-critical marketplace of contemporary U.S. fiction was going on Kathy Acker, Bret Easton Ellis, and David Foster Wallace. Although *The Counterlife* had received the best reviews of any Roth novel since *The Ghost Writer*, his status in 1990 was at best semi-canonical. By the time I finished my PhD, *Operation Shylock* and *Sabbath's Theater* had come out and Roth's stock was rising fast. By the time I got my first permanent teaching position, *American Pastoral* had won the Pulitzer Prize for fiction and people were talking about Roth as "America's greatest living novelist." By the time my monograph on him came out, this perception of his pre-eminence had hardened into something like a consensus.

I was pleased, of course, by Roth's success, not least, perhaps, for selfish reasons: my judgment had been implicitly vindicated, my research profile had been enhanced by the work that I had done on him, and once I became known as a leading Roth scholar, a virtuous circle of sorts was established: with each publication on Roth, and the resulting citations, I was commissioned to write further publications, which in turn consolidated my reputation and helped my career progress. But part of me also felt disappointed. Roth was never exactly a well-kept secret, but when I started working on him it was still perfectly possible to read every word that had been written on him, as well as by him. There was no Philip Roth Society, no *Philip Roth Studies*; there were no Philip Roth conferences. I felt about him as I once did about Fleetwood Mac, before they became trendy: that, while many people might have heard of him, few really knew his work well, and fewer still really appreciated the genius of the man—really *understood* his work, as I did. Once it became a truth (nearly) universally acknowledged that Roth was a great writer—possibly the greatest of his generation—I felt increasingly proprietorial, as though I wanted to reclaim something that had been lost. Just as, whenever I read of some new hipster band citing Fleetwood Mac as an influence, I want to ask them: have you actually ever listened to anything other than *Rumours?*, so with the ever-expanding critical discourse on Roth, I found myself asking: Who were these Johnny-come-latelys who were now jumping on the Roth bandwagon? And how authentic was their enthusiasm, how deep their knowledge? Had they read *When She Was Good? Our Gang?* "On the Air," "The Day it Snowed"? Or just *American Pastoral* and *The Human Stain?* This is, of course, ungenerous and unfair—I've written about authors without necessarily becoming thoroughly immersed in their life's work—but there it is.

Apart from speaking to the media on the day after Roth's death, the other thing the people in the press office at Reading got me to do was write a polemical piece for "The Conversation," in which I argued that "Philip Roth was the best post-war American writer, no ifs or buts." Predictably, this provoked a number of responses from readers, ranging from polite demurrals to howls of outrage and snorts of derision. Judging from the comments below the line, I needn't have worried that Roth had now become *too* popular. What was really interesting is that when I responded to these comments, conceding that my view—like any value judgement about any form of art—was, in the end, subjective, and politely inquiring which Roth novels the posters of the comments had actually read, a genuine conversation began. Instead of shrill claim and counter-claim, a number of us began exchanging recommendations of favorite novels and authors (some of whom *are* well-kept secrets). It turned out that most of those who had initially posted disparaging remarks about Roth had either read only one of his books or had more ambivalent views, having read one that they liked, for example, but then moved on to another that they had found disappointing and had not persisted. It was in the process of participating in this dialogue over a week or two that I recalled most vividly the things that had got me into Roth—and kept me hooked—over a period of more than three decades. I would like to finish by sharing some of these.

I first discovered Roth as an adolescent when I picked *Portnoy's Complaint* up at random from my parents' bookshelves (at that time I knew nothing of the divide between high and low culture, so that it was sandwiched, in my reading history, between Sidney Sheldon's *Bloodline* and Paul Gallico's *Too Many Ghosts*). In spite of the geographical and historical gap between the setting of the novel and the world in which I was growing up (North London in the 1980s), so much of the novel felt familiar, particularly the hilarious but queasy ambivalence of the Jewish protagonist towards his own Jewishness. I recall, in particular, reading the following passage, laughing so much that my stomach muscles ached, and then reading it out loud to all my Jewish friends, as well as to my parents.

"Do you remember Seymour Schmuck, Alex?" she asks me, or Aaron Putz or Howard Shlong, or some yo-yo I am supposed to have known in grade school twenty-five years ago, and of whom I have no recollection whatsoever. "Well, I met his mother on the street today, and she told me that Seymour is now the biggest brain surgeon in the entire Western Hemisphere. He owns six different split-level ranch-type houses made all of fieldstone in Livingston, and belongs to the boards of eleven synagogues, all brand-new and designed by Marc Kugel, and last year with his wife and his two little daughters, who are so beautiful that they are already under contract to Metro, and so brilliant that they should be in college—he took them all to Europe for an eighty-million-dollar tour of seven thousand countries, some of them you never even heard of, that they made them just to honor Seymour, and on top of that, he's so important, Seymour, that in every single city in Europe that they visited he was asked by the mayor himself to stop and do an impossible operation on a brain in hospitals that they also built for him right on the spot, and—listen to this—where they pumped into the operating room during the operation the theme song from *Exodus* so everybody should know what religion he is—and that's how big your friend Seymour is today! *And how happy he makes his parents!*" (*Portnoy* 99; italics in original)

This is essentially just one joke—and a familiar one at that—but its brilliance lies in the bathetic absurdity of the details (the synagogues designed by Marc Kugel, the *Exodus* theme song being piped into the operating theatre), the rhythms of the speech that so perfectly capture the inflections of second-generation Jewish immigrants ("that they made them just to honor Seymour [. . .] he's so important, Seymour [. . .] so everybody should know what religion he is") and the way that Roth continually cranks up the hyperbole, piling each increasingly outlandish claim on top of the preceding one to create a preposterous, but paradoxically compelling, chimerical *tour de force*.

Much as I had enjoyed *Portnoy's Complaint*, it was some years before I read any more Roth. This time it was *The Counterlife*, which I read in hardback when it first came out, after reading a review of it in *The London Review of Books* by Julian Barnes. By this time, I had a greater appreciation of what made literary fiction literary—earlier that year I had read *Anna Karenina*, *Madame Bovary* and the first volume of Proust—but I had never encountered anything like *The Counterlife*. It redefined for me what a novel could be, and do. When I finished it, I decided that I had to read everything else Roth had written. And yet, for all its dazzling twists and turns, its metaphysical conceits and metafictional games, the moments that stayed with me were the quiet, incidental details, such as the cameo appearance at Henry's funeral in "Basel" of the father of Henry's wife, Carol:

> While people were still crowding into the back of the synagogue and bridge chairs were found to seat some elderly latecomers, while there was nothing to do but sit in silence only feet away from the coffin deciding whether to keep looking at it or not, Bill Goff began rhythmically to make a fist and then undo it, opening and closing his right hand as though it were a pump with which to work up courage or to drain off fear. He barely resembled any longer the agile, sharp-dressing, spirited golfer that Zuckerman had first seen some eighteen years before, dancing with all the bridesmaids at Henry's wedding. Earlier that morning, when Goff had opened the door to let him in, Nathan hadn't even realized at first whose hand he was shaking. The only thing about him that looked undiminished was the full head of wavy hair. Inside the house, turning sadly to his wife—and sounding just a bit affronted—Goff had said to her, "How do you like that? He didn't even recognize me. That's how much I changed." (*Counterlife* 23)

In terms of the narrative of *The Counterlife* this paragraph is redundant: it does nothing to further the plot and we never see Bill Goff again. And yet, like so many of Shakespeare's bit parts (an analogy which in itself constitutes the highest praise), Goff springs to life off the page. The poignancy of his pique at the fact that Nathan fails to recognize him; the vivid idiomatic way, in which he expresses —half-jokingly, semi-seriously—his indignation; and the piercing acuity with which Roth captures the man's awkward, unconscious flexing of his hand, subtly echoed in the handshake with Nathan later in the passage, are all, to me, almost unbearably moving.

Finally, I recall the thrill of reading the opening sentences of *Sabbath's Theater*, with the conviction that this was a great writer at the absolute height of his powers:

> Either forswear fucking others or the affair is over.

> This was the ultimatum, the maddeningly improbable, wholly unforeseen ultimatum, that the mistress of fifty-two delivered in tears to her lover of sixty-four on the anniversary of an attachment that had with an amazing licentiousness—and that, no less amazingly, had stayed their secret—for thirteen years. But now with hormonal infusions ebbing, with the prostate enlarging, with probably no more than another few years of semi-dependable potency still his—with perhaps not that much

more life remaining—here at the approach of the end of everything, he was being charged, on pain of losing her, to turn himself inside out. (*Sabbath* 3)

Prose doesn't get much better than this. From the pithy audacity of the opening sentence, with its juxtaposition of formal and demotic registers, to the subtle play on degrees of possibility ("improbable . . . probably . . . perhaps . . ."), to the poignancy of Sabbath's predicament, with its combination of specific somatic symptoms of decline and more metaphysical intimations of mortality, to the masterly economy of the exposition: everything about this opening is peerless, pitch-perfect, at once unmistakably Rothian and at the same time inimitable and startling.

Passages such as these have of course been enjoyed by thousands of other readers; they do not belong to me anymore than they belong to anyone else. And yet they speak to me, perhaps, differently from the way in which they speak to others, in ways that make me profoundly grateful. Similarly, I have no special claim to Roth, no privileged access to his work, and yet I enjoy a particular relationship with it that is mine and mine alone. In that sense, I have my own private Philip Roth—one who will survive for as long as I do.

WORKS CITED

Roth, Philip, *Portnoy's Complaint*, Vintage, 2005.
---. *The Counterlife*, Vintage, 2005.
---. *Sabbath's Theater*, Vintage, 2010.

I am an American, Newark Born

Alan Cooper

Such an Augie March-like pronouncement might have spilled out of the mouths of Neil Klugman, Swede Levov, Nathan Zuckerman, Ira Ringold, Marcus Messner, and the "Philips" and "Roths" of their author's late-middle period and *The Plot Against America*. Might have, but never quite did, although they were all characters from Weequahic.

That Newark neighborhood, 96% Jewish, was, for Roth, a Zion of safety that rendered everywhere else, even Israel, diaspora. Perhaps we might include—briefly—Bradley Beach, Weequahic's summer extension on the Jersey shore. Include, that is, for families from Weequahic, who shared refrigerators, pantries, swim-suit changing rooms, Yiddish accents.

But being *from* Bradley Beach, a year-round off-season collection of ethnic flotsam and jetsam, would disqualify Morris [Mickey] Sabbath from feeling safe in that America, even though he'd wiggled his baby toes in the ripples of its eastern shore.

Safety was not Augie March's need. His was a buoyancy that carried him through his adventures wherever he went. He was an American before (if only in the womb) he was a Chicagoan. Roth's Weequahic Jews drew on the restorative blood of their womb-like birthplace to barely survive the challenges of the wider world.

Weequahic was more than a location within Newark: the smells of its cooking, the accents of its candy stores and ball fields, its steam baths, Roth's grandfather's shaving mug upon a shelf in the barber shop, these visceral associations—much more than any synagogue—created this paradise of Jewishness. Nathan Zuckerman, world traveler, might say, "I am never more of a Jew than when I am in a church when the organ begins. [. . .] I have the emotions of a spy in the adversary's camp" (*Counterlife* 256). Still, as Aharon Appelfeld would put it, "Roth's Jews are Jews without Judaism" (Alterman). Although his characters could precisely describe the dimensions of a proper Jewish grave, the dying Roth arranged to be buried on the secular campus of Bard College.

For how long can we speak of "the dying Roth"? Was it from the time he stopped publishing fiction? And how, if at all, did his withdrawal from publishing new works affect his ability to withstand the dying?

Roth had stopped writing fiction in 2009. It remained for the Library of America to publish his collected nonfiction some nine years later (*Why Write?: Collected Nonfiction*), reviewed early in March 2018[1] and excerpted in *Harper's Magazine* for August 2017 and then again as "Memento Mori" on May 23, 2018 (the day after Roth's death). Among the essays included is one in which Roth tells of his first experience as a writer, at age ten, during World War II. At the kitchen table his loving mother was teaching him to type on her old Underwood typewriter, and he started writing a sea story, *Storm Off Hatteras*, in imitation of Howard Pease, "the Joseph Conrad of boys' books." Where the author's name was to follow the title, he wrote "Eric Duncan," because, he said, "a name with two hard Cs" is bound to sound strong ("Eric Duncan," *Why Write?* 346).

Three years later, graduating from elementary school, in the first Weequahic class to have celebrated winning the war against anti-Semitism, he co-wrote a pageant-like morality play for graduation called *Let Freedom Ring* in the spirit of Frank Sinatra's "The House I Live In." The girl who had been chosen as his coauthor played its protagonist, *Tolerance*. Its antagonist, played by nearly thirteen-year-old Philip, was called *Prejudice*. The numerous ethnic and religious groups spread out across the stage could not see the protagonist or the antagonist, standing at the sides of the stage, but these groups were praised by *Tolerance* with quotations from the Declaration of Independence, the U.S. Constitution, and newspaper columns by Eleanor Roosevelt, and they were denounced by *Prejudice* in language and epithets that Roth would not have uttered in real life. It was his first experience of being bad—and "Secretly, it thrilled me to think I had a natural talent for it" ("Eric Duncan," *Why Write?* 347).

In essay after essay of *Why Write?* Roth reminds readers to be wary of the biographical fallacy and to steer clear of public-relations fictions like those of Leon Uris, which offer what the Jewish public wants, rather than, as Roth painfully provided, what the Jewish public knows. Over time he becomes convinced of what he merely speculated about early on, that fiction is no longer possible because the public mind has been overwhelmed by news so preposterous as to blunt any competition from the imagination.

But in January of 2017 he talked by email to *The New Yorker* about the newly elected president, Donald Trump. "It isn't Trump as a character, a human type—the real-estate type, the callow and callous killer capitalist—that outstrips the imagination. It is Trump as President of the United States." He called Trump "humanly impoverished [...] with a working vocabulary of seventy-seven words" and urged his fellow writers to keep speaking up (Thurman). Was this published email his new mode of *literature*, that catch-all word that had famously "got me into *this* and [. . .] is gonna to have to get me out" (*My Life* 195, italics added)?

Was Roth threatened by Trump—by a worse president than his own Tricky Dixon (*Our Gang*, 1971) and "The Uriah Heepism of [that] sweating president" (*Shop Talk* 139)? or worse than the twerp W—whose reelection he had his characters wait out on a late night in 2004 (*Exit Ghost*, 2007)? Could the reality of Trump prove fatal to the weakened and pulsating constitution of Philip Roth? Was his current "*this*" life itself?

When asked by *The New Yorker* for a piece about his current activity, he submitted part of an acceptance speech for the National Book Foundation's Medal for Distinguished Contribution to American Letters—written back in 2002. It was published in *The New Yorker's* "Life and Letters" column for June 5 & 12, 2017, as "I Have Fallen in Love with American Names," complete with a 1943 family picture of the Roths, when Philip was ten. But he adds to this family of four some early siblings he had personally adopted: Theodore Dreiser, Sherwood Anderson, Ring Lardner, Sinclair Lewis, Thomas Wolfe, and Erskine Caldwell, each born in a different state in the 1870s and 80s. He would be, above all else, an American.

Roth was born a half-century later than these added siblings. They were part of him as Washington and Lincoln were part of him, in his blood but not necessarily on his mind. He would not, as, say, E. L. Doctorow would, set his fictions in earlier eras to compile a kind of fictional context for American history, applying imagination to research. Roth's fiction is set within his own life span, usually a few years back, sometimes into his childhood. And he too would apply his imagination to his research—into the details of glove making, or watch making, or ice fishing. Roth's American trilogy may be read as a commentary on recent history, but it is, first of all, a set of novels, imaginatively realized.

However, as he had earlier explained, "[t]his butcher, imagination [. . .] clubs the fact over the head, [. . .] slits its throat, and [. . .] pulls forth the guts. [. . .] By the time the imagination is finished with a fact, believe me, it bears no resemblance to a fact. [. . .] To be sure, there cannot be anywhere, in all the realms of contemplation, anything so disgusting as the taste of a rotten book. But when it tastes good, gamey and good, there's nothing like it, is there?" ("This Butcher" 3).

Roth died on May 22, 2018.

On May 24th *The New York Times* published seven pieces on Roth: on page A1, an "Appraisal" by Dwight Garner called "A Born Spellbinder and a

Peerless Chronicler of Love and Death"; on page A27, a full–page essay by Joseph Berger, complete with a picture of Roth and friends at the Weequahic High School prom and a full-page headline announcing, "Twain Had His River, Roth Had Newark,"; on A28, a two-page biographic obituary with that 1943 photo of the Roth family and another of Roth in 2012; on A30, the Opinion [editorial] page, an "Appreciation" titled "Philip Roth's Earth-Moving Prose"; opposite that, on A30, an Op-Ed by Sam Lipsyte called—and defending—"Philip Roth's 'Toxic Masculinity'"; and, from a woman reader, a moving letter to the editor given the title, "Philip Roth's Genius, and His Humility," which includes the line, "He should have won the Nobel Prize"; finally, on C8, in its Arts and Leisure section, a page and a half called "Reading Philip Roth Over Time: a sampling of how critics viewed his work over time." This last piece, complete with book jackets, offers quotations from *New York Times* reviews of numerous books covering his many periods. The *Times* had just begun its celebration of Roth.

Two days later, the *Times* published an essay in its Arts section by a staff writer, a Jewish woman, Taffy Brodesser-Akner, who had been brought up within the confines of ultra (not ultra-ultra) Jewish orthodoxy, titled "Roth Taught Me the Way to Be a Jew." She cites several of his books to pinpoint different liberating elements. She concludes her essay,

> He was called self-hating for all this. But he wasn't self-hating. He was paving a road that would legitimize the American Jewish experience so thoroughly as to elicit a piece like this upon his death [. . .] he was affirming to us that we were contenders. Like our experiences deserved to be considered and judged.

> Like we belonged here.

The first strictly literary appreciation (of about 1200 words), by Cynthia Ozick, appeared in the on-line edition of *The Wall Street Journal* of May 25 (at 5:21 pm) as "Appreciation: Philip Roth," and in the print edition of May 26th, as "In Praise of Zest and Laughter." Ozick pretends to bolster the now-dead Roth's ego by listing him among other deserving writers who never won the Nobel Prize, notably Mark Twain, James Joyce, and Tolstoy. She calls him a "genie of biting comedy," a product of Jewish Weequahic. She supplies the well-known view that he was playful and serious, and, in her own inimitable fashion, the adjective *chthonic*, a word Roth would never have used.

New York magazine (May 28-June 10) had Roth on its Critics page in Christian Lorentzen's "The Infinite Philip Roth: 1933-2018," in which Lorentzen rejects the idea that Roth was merely "a product of his time." The genre of the novel, he insists, will not die with Roth, even if Roth thought it would. Most of the names filling the newspapers during Roth's life, Lorentzen says, "are lost to time, which will never be true of Alexander Portnoy, Nathan Zuckerman, Amy Bellette, or Mickey Sabbath." Indeed, Lorentzen tells us, "Roth probably contemplated death more than any writer after Tolstoy," but he leaves us characters like Mickey Sabbath, who "could not fucking die. [...] How could he go? Everything he hated was here" (*Sabbath* 451).

Still there were those who could not appreciate the impact of Roth's imagination on facts. In the Sunday Review of May 27th, the *New York Times* published an opinion piece by novelist Dara Horn called "Roth's Jewish Women." She claims to be the one person capable of correcting his distorted impression of that girl from *Goodbye, Columbus*,

> Brenda Patimkin, the Newark narrator's love interest. Vain and vapid, Brenda [...] had her nose "fixed" to fit in with her Harvard classmates. [...] I went to Brenda Patimkin's public [Short Hills] high school— which by the time I graduated in 1995 felt nearly as Jewish as Roth's Newark. Harvard was where I learned Yiddish.

> [...] But for my family the work of Philip Roth [...] was intimate and personal. Every restaurant, synagogue and cemetery in his books was a real location in my family's life. So how could this Jewish girl from Short Hills, and the many others like her that populate Roth's books, feel so unfamiliar? Despite the years that divided us, wasn't Brenda supposed to be a girl like . . . me? (final ellipsis in original)

Making her subject *herself* allows Horn to join #MeToo: she accuses Roth of demeaning women throughout his works. However, she has little appreciation of context. She cites Roth's favorite topics as Jews, women, and New Jersey, and calls Roth a virtuoso of mocking all three. Her evidence is phrases spoken by characters:

> "What are they, after all, these Jewish women who raised us up as children?" "It isn't their fault they were given a gift like speech—look, if cows could talk, they would say things just as idiotic. Yes, yes, maybe that's the solution then: think of them as cows, who have been given the twin miracles of speech and mah-jongg."

> [...] jokes like this [Horn insists] haven't aged well, yet they were just as cruel in 1969—and the misogyny isn't really the problem. [...] The problem is literary: these caricatures reveal a lack not only of empathy but also of curiosity.

Nineteen-sixty-nine! The quoted character is Alexander Portnoy spilling out his guts to Dr. Spielvogel. Yet for Horn it is all the same. Unlike Shakespeare on Shylock's pain or Twain on Huck's feelings for Jim, "Philip Roth's works are curious only about Philip Roth." But Horn misses completely the meaning of the second word in the two-word title. What is Portnoy's *Complaint*? It is not that he can't abuse women, but that he can't *enjoy* abusing them. He wants to be bad and guilt free, but he is bound by the precepts he learned from Sophie Portnoy—not from Bess Roth.

And lack of curiosity? What does Portnoy want from Spielvogel but answers to his endless questions? Portnoy doesn't know what Roth knew—that Roth's analyst had betrayed his profession by writing a disguised paper on a writer's analysis. So Roth allows Spielvogel to remain silent and to settle for his one-line zinger.

Moreover, Horn is writing her article in 2018, after the fictional Zuckerman's various Marias, after Sabbath's Drenka, after Bess Roth in *The Plot Against America*, and after Mrs. Messner in *Indignation*, all multi-dimensional female characters in Roth's post-*Portnoy* works.

Roth's life had been complicated by physical ailments, including a ruptured appendix, peritonitis, and a triple heart bypass. In his fiction he uses many of his ailments: the backache in "Novotny's Pain" and in *The Anatomy Lesson*, where Zuckerman settled for lying on the floor and being straddled by numerous women. Roth portrays four of them and gives each a real life and a motivation for the lowering. The fourth, Jaga, a defector from communist Poland, says, "I will let you do anything you want to me, but I will not fall in love. [. . . a writer is] interested in you mainly as a subject. Warm ice. I know writers" (*Zuckerman Bound* 538).

Roth had traveled in and out of Prague rescuing the works of "Writers from the Other Europe." He uses Prague to represent the whole communist east, where the general population had lost its soul, as the setting for that brilliant epilogue to *Zuckerman Bound*, "The Prague Orgy." Here Olga, "the writer with the best legs in Prague," (*Zuckerman Bound* 531) wants the vulnerable Zuckerman to get her out into the west—ostensibly, to rescue another manuscript of an unpublished piece of Jewish literature—or, temptingly, to rescue herself. Only by risking the danger of fictionalizing so close to the bone could Roth create the multi-dimensional Olga.

But in Dara Horn and countless other readers the biographical fallacy lives on. Vivian Gornick is quoted as having said, "If in Bellow misogyny was the seeping bile, in Roth it was lava pouring forth from a volcano" (Gornick 75).

But some writers knew better. The Newark Public Library instituted an *Annual Philip Roth Lecture* to be given by prominent writers. In October 2017 Roth invited Salman Rushdie to give the third annual lecture, which they scheduled for September 27, 2018. Rushdie, stunned by Roth's death, took the few remaining months to read all of Roth's works, and produced what may be the most comprehensive appreciation of novelists who risk including their own alienation as part of their emerging American voices (Rushdie).

So what, finally, is the meaning of life in Roth's later works? Old age is a "massacre." One is alive and then life stops. Much, much darker than the voice Bellow gives Augie in his final chapter: "Look at me, going everywhere!" (536). Perhaps we too should call Roth's work *chthonic*.

On May 22, 2018, Roth's life stopped. By his own lights, he can't pop up from the grave to object, any more than he can be hurt by the slings and arrows of Donald Trump.

At his grave site at Bard, according to the *New York Times*, there were three women in attendance, friends and writers, whose conversation included mention of sixteen stents surrounding his heart.

Maybe from a writer who has stopped publishing, a late email can be squeezed into his oeuvre as *literature*; but texting more about "the humanly impoverished" Donald Trump would not have saved Roth's life. Dying isn't the kind of "*this*" that literature can get one out of.

Sixteen stents! Blown! That would end the unwritten life.

ENDNOTES

1. See, for example, Nathaniel Rich.

WORKS CITED

Alterman, Eric. "The Death of Philip Roth's 'Lox and Bagels' Judaism." *The Nation*, 16-23 July 2018. https://www.thenation.com/article/death-philip-roths-lox -bagels-judaism/

Bellow, Saul. *The Adventures of Augie March*. 1953. Penguin, 1984.

Brodesser-Akner, Taffy. "What Philip Roth Taught Me About Being an American Jew." *New York Times*. 24 May 2018. https://www.nytimes.com/2018/05/24/books /philip-roth-jewish-education.html

Horn, Dara. "Roth's Jewish Women." *New York Times* 27 May 2018, p. SR2.

Gornick, Vivian. "Radiant Poison: Saul Bellow, Philip Roth, and the end of the Jew as Metaphor." *Harper's Magazine*. September, 2008, pp. 69-75.

Lorentzen, Christian. "The Infinite Philip Roth 1933-2018." *New York Magazine*, 28 May-10 June 2018, pp. 102, 104.

Rich, Nathaniel. "Roth Agonistes." Review of Philip Roth, *Why Write?: Collected Non-fiction 1960-2013. New York Review of Books*, 18 March 2018.

Roth, Philip. *The Counterlife*. Penguin, 1986.

---. *My Life as a Man*. Vintage, 1974.

---. *Sabbath's Theater*. Houghton, 1995.

---. *Shop Talk*. Vintage, 2001.

---. "This Butcher, Imagination: Beware of Your Life When a Writer's at Work." *New York Times Book Review*, 14 Feb. 1988, p. 3.

Rushdie, Salman. "How Philip Roth Became a Political Prophet." *Forward*, 3 October 2018. https://forward.com/culture/411296/salman-rushdie-how-philip-roth-became-a-political-prophet/

Thurman, Judith. "Philip Roth E-mails on Trump." *New Yorker*, 30 January 2017. https://www.newyorker.com/magazine/2017/01/30/philip-roth-e-mails-on-trump

"Invariably the prelude to missing the point"

Philip Roth, Mickey Sabbath, and Me

David Gooblar

I spent the second half of my twenties writing a book on Philip Roth. The book, which began as my PhD dissertation, was a study of Roth's literary career, from its beginnings in the late fifties up to the end of the twentieth century. Of course, Roth's career did not end at the end of the twentieth century. In fact, as I wrote my study, Roth kept writing, too. When I began in late 2003, he had published twenty-five books. By the time my book came out in 2011, that number had swelled to thirty-one. My subject wouldn't keep still.

So I needed to draw lines, to limit the project's scope in some way. The turn of the century seemed a good endpoint: both for the round number, and for the growing sense that Roth's "American Trilogy," which culminated with 2000's *The Human Stain*, would be the defining achievement of Roth's late-career resurgence. I couldn't have an open-ended study, expanding every time Roth published a new work. So, with the blessing of Kasia Boddy, my exceedingly wise PhD supervisor, I planned out a study of Roth's fiction, beginning with *Goodbye, Columbus* (1959) and concluding with *The Human Stain*. I could always briefly touch on the twenty-first-century work in the conclusion.

But even within those defined limits, I couldn't write about everything. Forty-one years in a career as productive as Roth's was more than a single dissertation could comprehensively cover. Writing is selection; the choices I would make about what books to cover would make a statement about their significance. In crafting the book's focus, especially after I decided to title the book *The Major Phases of Philip Roth*, I was making an argument. Here are the peaks of Roth's career, the books that make the biggest contribution to literary history, the books that are in some way representative of his entire achievement.

To tell the truth, I don't remember why exactly I left out *Sabbath's Theater*. The 1995 novel is a masterpiece, one of Roth's best, and that was clear to me as soon as I first read it in 2004. When I look back through my notes, I can find a number of prospective chapter plans, some laughably unrealistic. One potential plan included ten chapters—*Sabbath* was to be covered in the eighth. Once I settled on six chapters, the final chapter was to be focused on all of Roth's work from *Sabbath* forward. But somewhere along the way the book disappeared, and that sixth chapter turned into a reading of the American Trilogy alone.

What I do remember is always being self-conscious about the omission. I knew that a study of Roth's work with any ambitions of completeness had to reckon with Mickey Sabbath, and that any serious Roth scholar would glance at my table of contents and know that I was a fraud. The only mention of the novel in my completed dissertation is a footnote in the sixth chapter that Freud would have jumped all over: "For reasons of space, I will not take up Roth's *Sabbath's Theater* (1995) in this thesis, although it is undoubtedly one of his best works. Happily, there has been much excellent work on the novel in recent years; see" etc., etc. The footnote was not keyed to any particularly relevant discussion in the main text; it was a sheepish attempt to justify the unjustifiable, to let readers know that I knew there was something missing, while suspiciously eliding the fact that it was I who chose to leave it out.

When I turned the dissertation into a book, I conceivably had the chance to revise its contents, to expand my study, to grapple with *Sabbath's Theater* and integrate it into my readings of the other books. But for one reason or another (my publisher was happy with the original manuscript; I was always busy with other projects), I didn't do it. Even the exculpatory footnote disappeared.

***

How to sum up *Sabbath's Theater*? You could do worse than to begin by quoting the novel's first line: "Either forswear fucking others or the affair is over" (3). The whole novel lives in this sentence: the conflict between indulging impulses and controlling them; the bald obscenity; the sense of life as a series of intolerable choices; the unceasing presence of an ending; the delight in both high-flown language (*forswear* appears in Shakespeare at least thirty times) and the directness of the spoken word. Roth had been including the word *fuck* in his novels since 1962's *Letting Go*, and the second excerpt of *Portnoy's Complaint* memorably began with an explicit description of masturbation ("Then came the years when half my waking life was spent locked behind the bathroom door, firing my wad down the toilet"), but the directness here, the seriousness with which the book's opening takes transgression, signals a different kind of book than Roth had been writing ("Whacking Off" 385). I've been rereading the book as I work on this piece, perhaps my fifth time reading it straight through, and I still can't really get my head around it or make sense of its place within Roth's œuvre.

The novel belongs to Mickey Sabbath in much the same way that the books of *Zuckerman Bound* belong to Nathan Zuckerman, in much the same way that most of Roth's books prior to the American Trilogy belong to their protagonist-narrators. But while there are superficial similarities between Sabbath and earlier Roth alter egos (he was born during the Depression, pursues an artistic vocation, has an intense connection to his mother, thinks about sexual desire constantly), the way we follow Sabbath, from his affair with Drenka Balich, to his torpedoing of his marriage, to his return to the streets of New York, and then eventually to the Jersey shore of his childhood, I find dizzying, disorienting, more difficult to digest than Roth's other books.

Roth's books, as far back as *Portnoy's Complaint*, have long gained their power from the energy of the human voice, the magnetism of a man (it's always a man) attempting to shape the world with his words. Roth famously said that this quality was what made his books Jewish; it's "above all the *talking*. The talking and the shouting. Jews will go on, you know. It isn't what it's talking *about* that makes a book Jewish—it's that the book won't shut up" ("Interview" 140, italics in original). Maybe the difference here is that much of Sabbath's talking is going on inside his head. There are, as always, some juicy conversations, as when Sabbath attempts to seduce Michelle Cowan ("Behold the arrow of desire!" [336]). But the majority of Sabbath's talking is directed inward, and the result is claustrophobic, overwhelming in its intensity, as Sabbath careens deeper and deeper into his past while keeping one eye fixed on the future that awaits us all.

Death pervades the novel. The dead haunt Sabbath—his brother Morty, his mother, his first wife Nikki, Drenka, his friend Lincoln Gelman—and he spends much of the book thinking about suicide. Although death hangs over most of Roth's late work, nowhere else does it receive such thorough treatment. Sabbath curses death, longs for death, jokes about death, prepares for death, thinks about it endlessly. What death has to offer Sabbath he hints at when he is first visited by the ghost of his mother, who appears over Sabbath's shoulder while he is having sex with Drenka in their secluded grotto: "his tiny dynamo of a mother was now beyond all taboos" (29). Sabbath's life has been a war waged against taboos, be they sexual, artistic, social, or hygienic. In that, he is in a long line of Roth figures, bridling at the limits that conscience, or parents, or religion, or puritanism, put on desire.

"To be bad—and to enjoy it!" was the impossibility that Alexander Portnoy supposedly wanted above all else (*Portnoy* 124). For a writer famous for his transgressions on the page, Roth's writing about such transgressions was always in the context of the good son, the serious and moral young man raised to do the right thing—which is to repress. To sin is only interesting if there's a rabbi, or a mother, or an internalized moral code telling you to stop. Discussing his writing process for the outrageous and often baffling *The Great American Novel*, Roth described his forays into absurd fantasy as flouting his internal critic and judge: "When the censor in me rose responsibly in his robes to say, 'Now look here, don't you think that's just a little too—' I would reply, from beneath the baseball cap I often wore when writing that book, 'Precisely why it stays! Down in front!'" ("After" 96-97). I think Roth needed that censor, needed that voice in his head telling him what to do and what not to do, to rebel against.

For Sabbath, the whole world serves as a foil. Sabbath defines himself by the strictures of society that he dodges, proud of being unimpeded by those conventions that exist to impede everyone. When, late in the novel, he attempts to urinate on Drenka's grave, and initially finds it impossible, he briefly worries that he has been caught at last, run down and tackled by the forces he's been evading his whole life:

> Could what was impeding the urine flow be that wall of conscience that deprives a person of what is most himself? What had happened to his entire conception of life? It had cost him dearly to clear a space where he could exist in the world as antagonistically as he liked. Where was the contempt with which he had overridden their hatred; where were the laws, the code of conduct, by which he had labored to be free from their stupidly harmonious expectations? Yes, the strictures that had inspired his buffoonery were taking their vengeance at last. All the taboos that seek to abate our monstrosity had shut his water down. (444)

Here, then, is the extremity of Mickey Sabbath: "his entire conception of life" hinges on whether or not he will be able to piss on his lover's grave. Luckily for Sabbath, and for us, this is only a momentary difficulty; the water comes, the dark cloud passes, and Sabbath ends the book as anarchic and countersuggestive as ever.

***

When Roth died this past May, I mourned the man first. But then, of course, I started thinking about the man's work, the oeuvre. And I tried to make sense of it all, the incredible run of books, the incredible *range* Roth covered while always remaining unmistakeably himself. But there it still was, sticking out like a sore thumb. *Sabbath's Theater*.

In my book's introduction, I argued that "even some of the best critical work on Roth has tended to overlook the ways in which Roth's career frustrates most attempts at imposing unity" (4). I was trying to clear a space for my work, trying to distinguish my thesis from everybody else's. Ultimately what I tried to argue was that Roth's central quality, at least if you're trying to sum up all of the work, is his slipperiness. It was a sort of anti-thesis, an argument that Roth will make any thesis look foolish in time. I quoted, admiringly, Mark Shechner's great line: "Roth does what he does because he does what he does" (Shechner 4).

But of course, even as he paid tribute to the inexplicability of Roth's work, Shechner filled pages and pages with explanations and interpretations of Roth. It's what we do. It's what I did, too. To spend as much time with Roth's books as I have, as all of us who write about Roth have, is to seek to make sense of the books, to find patterns and make them visible, to distill meaning. Roth wrote that Mickey Sabbath "was reduced the way a sauce was reduced, boiled down by his burners, the better to concentrate his essence and be defiantly himself" (126). Could critical writing about Sabbath further reveal his concentrated essence? Or is the only possible result a reduced Sabbath in another sense: lessened, flattened, a shadow of his former self? I wonder if it was fear of this sort of reduction that lay behind my omission of *Sabbath's Theater*: if I wrote about the book, if I shoehorned it in my grand unified theory of Philip Roth, I'd inevitably spoil its magic.

As I look over my observations about *Sabbath's Theater* above—the explication of the opening line, the theorizing about voice in the novel, the connection between death and taboo, Roth's interest in conscience and transgression—I'm left with an empty feeling. This is a kind of thinking about literature that comes to me as naturally as reading itself. But I can't help but feel that such thinking misses the point. I often think about something Roth said to David Remnick, when the latter asked him what he thought about academic interpretations of his work. Roth asks Remnick to imagine a father taking his son to a baseball game, and instead of showing the kid what's happening on the field, he keeps the kid's attention on the scoreboard. They watch the scoreboard together, and cheer when the numbers change, keeping track of how many times they changed. "Is that politicizing the baseball game? Is that theorizing the baseball game?" Roth asks Remnick. "No, it's having not the foggiest idea in the world what baseball is" (Remnick 86).

I don't agree with Roth's sweeping generalizations about literary criticism's pointlessness, but I will say that *Sabbath's Theater* makes me feel the pointlessness of meaning-making. "That unaccountable exaggeration, significance: in Sabbath's experience invariably the prelude to missing the point" (378). For me at least, the book is critic-proof. There's something bewildering about the book, something ultimately mysterious and sublime that leaves me as disoriented as I would be standing on the deck of a merchant marine ship with Mickey Sabbath himself. Sure, I can note that Sabbath is a man at war with taboos, and I can notice that Roth's heroes often struggle against restrictions that they halfway believe in. I can dance the interpretive dance. But if I try to put into words the power of the book's last hundred pages, the way Roth sends Sabbath to hell and back, only to leave him washed up on the Shore, his Shore, to convene with his dead, I fall short.

Whether Philip Roth is now beyond all taboos I cannot say. But for those of us still here, those of us still reading and thinking about Roth, and writing about all that he wrote, I like the thought that *Sabbath's Theater* can exist as a reminder of all that is untameable, unassimilable, in his work. For all that the past twenty years has brought us an explosion of amazing work on Roth, for all that I have enjoyed and benefitted from the critics who have taken Roth as seriously as he deserves to be taken, I'm glad of a reminder that Roth can't be finally figured out, can't be exhausted. Such a reminder seems, paradoxically, to guarantee that there will be more great writing about Roth to come. For me though, I'm going to be content to merely wonder at Roth for a bit. I'd like to reread the books without always looking to draw conclusions, to find patterns, to pin the books down. I'd like simply to be in the hands of a master, to experience that pleasure, to live with the reality he conjures up.

WORKS CITED

Gooblar, David. *The Major Phases of Philip Roth.* Continuum, 2011.

Remnick, David. "Into the Clear." *The New Yorker,* 8 May 2000, pp. 76-89.

Roth, Philip. "After Eight Books." *Reading Myself and Others.* Vintage, 2001, pp. 85-97.

---. "Interview with *The Paris Review.*" *Reading Myself and Others.* Vintage, 2001, pp. 119-48.

---. *Portnoy's Complaint.* Vintage, 1999.

---. *Sabbath's Theater.* Vintage, 1996.

---. "Whacking Off." *Partisan Review,* vol. 34, Summer, 1967, pp. 385-99.

Shechner, Mark. *Up Society's Ass, Copper.* U of Wisconsin P, 2003.

Meeting Philip Roth

Jay L. Halio

"You know more about me than my mother," Philip said, as I greeted him at Wilmington's train station. As acting director of Delaware's Jewish Studies program, I had invited him to our campus to give a talk or a reading in spring of 1993. We needed someone outstanding as a visiting speaker, and as I had recently completed my book about him and his work, who else could I think of but him?

I took Philip to the Hilton Hotel, where we had lunch together and he had a room for the night. At lunch I found Philip very easy to talk to, and we enjoyed a few laughs together. All this came at a time when rumor had it that that he was having a nervous breakdown and going through a divorce from Claire Bloom after fifteen years of living together and three years of marriage. From all I could tell, Philip looked and sounded perfectly normal—not a hint of any psychological disorder (despite what Claire Bloom says in *Leaving a Doll's House* [1996]), so I did not bring up the subject. But I did ask him if the rumor was true about the divorce. He nodded to indicate it was, and I said I hoped it was an amicable divorce. He said it wasn't, and I immediately dropped the subject.

That evening I could not persuade Philip to have dinner with me and a few colleagues before his presentation, though I suspect he might have had a bite on his own, either before or after the event. I was somewhat surprised that he chose to read from *Patrimony*, which had recently been published, instead of one of his novels or stories, but I was very glad he did. It is, of course, one of the best things he has written, and he read from it beautifully. When he agreed to answer questions from the audience after he spoke, he introduced an innovation. He asked that the audience write down their questions on slips of paper that were given out. I assumed naturally that he wanted to screen the questions, but he informed me later that this was a technique to prevent people from standing up and speaking endlessly before they got to their questions. The device worked very well, I have to admit, and after reading for about forty-five minutes, he began answering some of the questions he had selected.

One of the questions still stands out vividly in my mind. Someone asked, "When you write, do you think of yourself as an American writer or a Jewish writer?" His answer was what we should have expected. He said, "When I write, I ask myself what is wrong with this sentence, and how can I correct it?" What better answer could he—or any writer—give to the kind of question asked? Most of us know that Philip's books go through a number of revisions, often many, before he feels they are ready to see print. It is no wonder that stylistically as well as in other ways he is one of the best writers in America since World War II.

I cannot recall many of the other questions, but one of them referred to a restaurant in New York that was a favorite of Philip's. Both he and the questioner enjoyed a good laugh about that, and I wish I could remember exactly what the question was and what occasioned the laughter. In any case, Philip was in excellent form and generously continued to answer questions for many minutes afterwards.

We held a reception for Philip Roth later but advised those who came that it was not for signing books. Philip, who had been on his feet for about two hours, was understandably reluctant to stay long, disappointing the president of our University and others. The next morning I drove him to the airport, but before I let him out of the car, I did ask him to sign a few of his books I brought along. After all, how could I resist such an opportunity? I included the book I wrote about him, which I was sure he read since he signed it by using one of the quotations from someone I mentioned in the book. "Tour de farce indeed," he wrote, but earlier when I finally got the courage to ask him what he thought of my book, he said simply, "It's a good book." And that was good enough for me.

I met Philip on several other occasions. One of them was at the Folger Shakespeare Library where he was awarded a prize for *Operation Shylock* as the best novel of the year. In the book he dwelt somewhat on the controversial trial in Jerusalem of a man accused of crimes against victims of the Holocaust. The jury in Israel acquitted the man, but Philip muttered to me, "He was guilty," as indeed I and many others also believed.

Another occasion was when he returned to Wilmington to receive one of the Commonwealth prizes that were awarded that evening. Before the dinner and the award ceremony, I was invited to meet with Philip and the other notable guests receiving awards. While most of them were standing holding their drinks and chatting with each other, Philip stayed seated on a couch. That was the first indication I had that his health was not exactly robust. At the dinner, when each awardee was asked to say a few words, Philip typically said he didn't know what he was doing there when he should be back home working on his next book.

I hope this brief memoir gives readers some idea of the kind of man Philip was. His eightieth birthday celebration was held partly in the public library in Newark, N.J., where Philip had worked as a young man, much like Neil Klugman in "Goodbye, Columbus." It was a two-day affair that included a day of reading papers on Roth's oeuvre, a tour of the neighborhood where the Roth family lived and Philip went to public school, and a visit to the library's exhibition of photographs and other memorabilia, later published as a book. At the end of the occasion, Philip appeared to cut his birthday cake and greet a great many of the friends and others who came to help him celebrate. They crowded around him and shook hands—a testimony not only to Roth's great accomplishment as a writer, but I believe also as a very good man.

ARTICLE

Philip Roth and Pleasure

Patrick Hayes

William Wordsworth's Preface to the *Lyrical Ballads* is in no sense an aesthete's charter, nor do we tend to think of Wordsworth himself as a hedonist. But this writer, who did perhaps more than anyone to establish modern literature as an object of serious attention and human importance, nonetheless insisted that its primary function is to give "immediate pleasure," and that pleasure itself is no less than the "grand elementary principle" of our lives. Any form of writing that forgets this fact, Wordsworth insisted, will quickly become irrelevant.[1]

The question of irrelevance was on everyone's mind in a seminar I attended in Boston a few years ago, the aim of which was to reflect upon the crisis in literary studies in America. Falling enrollments, cuts in funding, and a sense of becoming ever more peripheral: these were our concerns. It was led by two scholars who had both published well-received academic books on postwar literature: one was about the institutional and economic environment of contemporary writing; the other dealt with the relationship between literature and human rights discourse. Neither of these thoughtful and intelligent books was animated by the idea that pleasure is the "grand elementary principle" that should inform our attention to literature at its deepest level. And as the seminar developed, there was an absence of the word "pleasure," or any of its cognates. Instead, the discussion was very much in keeping with the broadly sociological emphasis of the "Post-45" group of scholars, who are currently setting the direction of contemporary American literary studies.[2]

By contrast, pleasure is very emphatically something that Philip Roth did not forget about. It might even be said that his fiction rubs our noses in it. From Alexander Portnoy's frantic pursuit of sexual gratification, to Mickey Sabbath's delirious mockery of all moral values, Roth was intent on showing us that pleasure matters. He refused, to quote another of his characters, to "deodorize life and make it palatable" (*Communist* 179), insisting we confront the most embarrassing aspects of our humanity. And while Roth remains a very popular writer, he has often been marginalized and treated with suspicion by academic literary studies in America—that profession which now finds itself in crisis, with falling enrollments and a sense of becoming ever more peripheral.

Of course Wordsworth himself would hardly have recognized Roth's conception of pleasure, let alone hailed him as the savior of literary value. In the Preface to the *Lyrical Ballads* the experience of pleasure is understood via David Hartley's pantheistic psychology as a route to our best selves, and in some ways *The Prelude* affirms this view: its main narrative suggests that nature teaches us through pleasurable encounters with the beautiful and the sublime, and that poetry recaptures and intensifies those experiences, deepening that process of education.[3] As I have argued elsewhere, Roth's significance lies not least in the way his writing challenges this redemptive view of life—or more precisely, the assumption that our life is in need of any sort of redemption. Instead there is a distinctively Nietzschean orientation in his work, a tendency to conceive pleasure in a more explicitly vitalistic and embodied way as a love of intensities, of those qualitatively rich forms of becoming that Nietzsche called the "will to power" (his own name for that "grand elementary principle").

But while there is much to separate Roth and Wordsworth, they are united in the view that pleasure is in the deepest sense not a form of hedonistic dissipation but a special type of intelligence, and that one of the most primary things literature can do is educate us about it. Education was one of Roth's most enduring concerns, and among the many educators portrayed in his fiction one of the most memorable is Murray Ringold, the high school English teacher featured in *I Married a Communist*. Zuckerman remembers feeling "in the sexual sense, the power of a male high school teacher like Murray Ringold—masculine authority uncorrected by piety" (*Communist* 2). Yet Mr. Ringold's interest in power resides not in crude forms of domination, but in enabling his students to access their own pleasure-giving potency:

> Mr. Ringold knew very well [Zuckerman recalls] that what boys like me needed to learn was not only how to express themselves with precision and acquire a more discerning response to words, but how to be rambunctious without being stupid, how not to be too well concealed or too well behaved, how to begin to release the masculine intensities from the institutional rectitude that intimidated the bright kids the most. (2)

"How to be rambunctious without being stupid": this is a great lesson to learn, and Ringold teaches it through Shakespeare. Zuckerman recalls his memory of an English lesson on the end of Act IV of *Macbeth*, "when Macduff learns from Ross that Macbeth has slain Macduff's family." He remembers Mr. Ringold "doing all the voices, not afraid to be dramatic and perform"; he dwells on the particular moment at which Macduff, having been told, in the wake of such news, to "Dispute it like a man" (314), agrees that he must do so:

Then the simple line that would assert itself, in Murray Ringold's voice, a hundred times, a thousand times, during the remainder of my life: "But I must also feel it like a man." "Ten syllables," Mr Ringold tells us the next day, "That's all. Ten syllables, five beats, pentameter . . . nine words, the third iambic stress falling perfectly and naturally on the fifth and most important word . . . eight monosyllables and the one word of two syllables a word as common and ordinary and serviceable as any there is in everyday English . . . and yet, all together, and coming where it does, what power! Simple, simple—and like a hammer!" (314-15)

Mr. Ringold's way of reading throws contemporary approaches to literary studies into sharp relief. His demonstration of the way in which pleasure combines with intelligence discloses a very different notion of literature's human relevance.

If we dwell on this scene for just a little longer, it becomes clear that the intelligence of the "simple line" Ringold quotes lies at least partly in the capacities for powerful self-creation it unfolds for Zuckerman. It would echo with him "a hundred times, a thousand times, during the remainder of my life" (314), Zuckerman explains, enlarging and enriching his capacity for experience. But the deeper intelligence of this Shakespearean pleasure lies in its transgressiveness. What it transgresses against is the "faith in antithetical values," as Nietzsche called it: the naïve moralistic belief that values are separable and opposed, rather than being intertwined and interdependent (Nietzsche 159). Here Zuckerman gains access, through the line's sudden rush of pleasurable power, to the intuition that grief can be a state of strength rather than (as we often think of it) vulnerability; that this traditionally feminine quality can inhabit the most masculine of identities; that far from being enfeebling it can hit like a hammer. He learns that the quality of Macduff's grief turns on its relation to power; the richness of his seeming weakness comes through its relation to an indirect form of violence. It is in this way, Zuckerman implies, that literature engages us ethically: by exploring the way in which values and actions are, to some extent at least, a function of the quality and vitality with which they are performed. To put the same point a little more formally, Roth's fiction reminds us that literature can be a space in which the normative judgments we reach for through moral philosophy become entangled with aesthetic ones—that is to say, with judgments that are singular in their nature, and based on more intuitive forms of insight.

"To be rambunctious without being stupid": a great lesson perhaps, but Nietzsche's attempt to connect value judgments with the will to power has the potential to make us very stupid indeed, as the more misguided of his twentieth-century followers have amply demonstrated. I point this out only to emphasize that Roth's work should be read very precisely in Murray Ringold's terms: as a way of reckoning with Nietzsche's legacy that avoids stupidity, including moral stupidity. His fiction does not simply embody the will to power: it reflects upon its possibilities and limits. Roth's great theme is the collision between values established through sheer pleasurable intensity and more normative forms of moral reckoning, and his greatest writing explores this enormous subject with all the quizzical complexity it demands. *The Human Stain*, for example, invites us to place Coleman Silk's inspiringly Shakespearean self-conception against other forms of pleasure, perhaps most intriguing among which is a disturbing fascination with ecstatic self-loss: this appears to Coleman in his relationship with Faunia, and is further impressed upon readers in Zuckerman's oddly entrancing descriptions of the life lived by cows and crows. By remembering and foregrounding, rather than trying to forget or cover over, its relationship to the "grand elementary principle of pleasure," novels such as this one are able to open up unusually venturesome and complex ways of thinking.

But of course Roth cannot really be understood through a comparison with a well-meaning high school English teacher like Murray Ringold. Central to his emphasis on pleasure is a delight in outrage that would have had him kicked out of the academy. His writing bedevils small-mindedness; it mocks and derides the *agélastes*, to borrow a term coined by Rabelais—a writer with whom Roth has a certain long-distance affinity. An *agélaste*, explains Milan Kundera (one of Roth's most engaging correspondents), is "a man who does not laugh, who has no sense of humor," and as a group the *agélastes* are naturally suspicious of literature, convinced that "the truth is obvious [. . .] and that they themselves are exactly who they think they are" (*Art of the Novel* 159). "No peace is possible between the novelist and the *agélaste*," Kundera claims, and from the troublingly funny tape-recording of an anti-Semitic rant in *Operation Shylock*, to the lengthy transcription of phone-sex in *Sabbath's Theater*, Roth plays havoc with the straight lines of conventional seriousness, calling out the *agélastes* among us. His fiction includes everything we normally want to exclude from educative conversations about literature, insinuating all the while that our highest aspirations tend to be rather interestingly entangled with the more embarrassing sides of life. And of course this longstanding and unrepentant interest in unsettling the stale proprieties that find their way into both academic literary culture and contemporary moral discourse may well have been what cost him the Nobel Prize.

In its mockery of any form of normalizing institution, from high-school English teaching to psychiatric care, *Sabbath's Theater* is surely Roth's greatest work of outrage. But what is most memorable in this uniquely offensive book is not the raw directness with which it refuses to "deodorize life and make it palatable," but the pathos and strange beauty that emerge when the "grand elementary principle of pleasure" tears down our most primary ideas about how to distinguish what is shallow from what is deep. In the love affair between Drenka Balich and Mickey Sabbath, Roth shows how the most profound tenderness, and even wonder, can emerge in the very silliest human antics. At the tragic climax of the novel, driving back from the New Jersey shore, Sabbath starts to remember watching Drenka die. Consider, to end with, Drenka's own reminiscence of how they would urinate on each other in the woods:

> "It came down, and as it came upon me, I realized that it was warm. Do I dare to taste it? And I started with my tongue to lick around my lips. And there was this piss. And the whole idea that you were standing above me, and at first you strained to get it out, and then suddenly came this enormous piss, and it just came into my face and it was warm and it was just fantastic; it was exciting and everywhere and it was like a whirlwind, what I was feeling, the emotions." (*Sabbath* 425)

In the strange grace of Drenka's malapropism, intensified by the anguish of her cancer-riddled body, Sabbath's piss doesn't just come down: instead, "it came upon me," a phrase that in literary English carries the force of a religious revelation. She goes on, explaining that "I wanted everything of it, I wanted it on my tits," here confusing the word "everything" with its near-equivalent "all": what she really wanted was "all of it," as in every last drop. Yet in the pratfall of her malapropism, the combination of the wrong word ("everything") with the right preposition ("of") sends us stumbling into a quite different meaning. To want "everything of" Sabbath's piss in this moment opens onto a glimpse of love at its most radiant.

We are a long way from Wordsworth here—even though Roth's interest in malapropism resonates with the earlier writer's deployment of the mangled English used by idiots and beggars in the *Lyrical Ballads*. Yet *Sabbath's Theater* opens up another, now distinctively religious, dimension of what it means to value literary pleasure, which Wordsworth would certainly recognize and affirm. It is the capacity to be humbled before life: for a work of art to evoke so powerfully what is astonishing and surpassing within experience, that it generates a mood of reverence and awe. In *King Lear* Shakespeare needed the whole drama of a lost kingdom and a stormy heath to articulate this form of the sublime. In *Sabbath's Theater* all Roth needed was a couple of old perverts and a stream of warm piss.

NOTES

1. Wordsworth defines the "poet's art" as "a homage paid to the grand elementary principle of pleasure, by which he knows, and feels, and lives, and moves." *Lyrical Ballads*, p. 33.

2. "Post-45" is a group of scholars working on postwar American literature and culture: see http://post45.research.yale.edu

3. There are of course very different ways of reading this complex poem: see, for example, Paul de Man's essay on Wordsworth, "Autobiography as De-facement."

WORKS CITED

de Man, Paul. "Autobiography as De-facement." *The Rhetoric of Romanticism*, Columbia UP, 1983, pp. 67-82.

Kundera, Milan. *The Art of the Novel*, translated by Linda Asher, Faber, 1988.

Nietzsche, Friedrich. *Beyond Good and Evil*, translated by R. J. Hollingdale, Penguin, 1985.

Roth, Philip. *I Married a Communist*. Houghton, 1998.

---. *Sabbath's Theater*. Houghton, 1995.

Wordsworth, William. *Lyrical Ballads*, edited by Derek Roper, Northcote House, 1987.

How Many Feminists Does It Take to Screw in a Light Bulb?

Brett Ashley Kaplan

You may not believe this, but *Portnoy's Complaint* is my favorite Roth novel (followed closely by *Sabbath's Theater, Operation Shylock, Plot Against America,* and *The Human Stain*). As a feminist, it's quite a confession to avow that three of my favorites contain some of the most problematic women characters and most excessive and zany sexual content of any in contemporary Jewish American literature. But the truth is that some of Roth's women characters embody what would be called much later "consent culture"; they actively express unbounded desires in ways that crack open certain expectations that, some recent commentators like Kitty Stryker and Laurie Penny argue, paradoxically can fuel rape culture.[1] While The Monkey unfortunately still embodies the virgin/whore dichotomy and still maintains the stark divide in Roth and other writers' work wherein smart women are hardly ever sexy and sexy women are hardly ever smart, her character is to be credited with offering ample consent. It is definitely frustrating to be a feminist reader of Roth, and it is difficult to enjoy the *jouissance* of his writing and simultaneously be so distraught by the representations of women. Many of the major female characters (most of them not Jewish) are flattened, nicknamed, and objectified—it can be hard to celebrate the gems. I feel tossed between the utter joy of the prose (whatever else you might want to say about Roth, you have to hand it to him: he could write!) and the melancholia of seeing women debased. Only a smattering of women, including Steena from *The Human Stain*, are smart *and* voluptuous and pretty, so there remains a fairly unbreachable divide in Roth's novels between the smart and the sexy women. The Monkey is definitely sexy, not smart. Or rather, her intelligence is entirely embodied.

As we try to sift through Roth's legacy now that, sadly, there won't be any more novels, Roth's readers can square the enjoyment of his stunning prose with the problematics of the representation of women and thus find a space between the rock of appearing like a self-hating Jewish woman and the hard place of seeming like a joyless prude through close reading. Once you dig up the granular nuances of the text you'll see that, yes, there's a lot to object to, but there is also a complex critique of the troubling depictions embedded in the novels—their latent content might surprise you. Looking closely, there are through-the-looking-glass moments that counter the quick dismissal of Roth as "misogynist."

By focusing on The Monkey, I demonstrate how Roth's return to William Butler Yeats's "Leda and the Swan" at the end of *Portnoy's Complaint* (1969), where Portnoy takes the structural position of Leda, uncovers the anxieties of Jewish masculinity. By revisiting The Monkey, I argue that through Roth's contrasting representations of women, and through their broadcasting of Portnoy and his problems, Roth exposes the trouble with Jewish masculinity as much as he denigrates Portnoy's various consorts. Roth satirizes Portnoy to the same degree as he does The Monkey, or The Pumpkin, or The Jewish Pumpkin. But I would like to have my cake and eat it, too: just because the Jewish joke extends to the main male character, that does not mean that the representations of women are without major pitfalls. By unveiling the highly gendered problematics of the interactions between the men and women in this text (there are some queer moments but the overall arc is very heterosexual) Roth offers a nuanced reading of power dynamics that comes to a head during the reversed "Leda and the Swan" closing, where Portnoy becomes the victim and Naomi, the Israeli soldier, The Jewish Pumpkin, becomes Zeus.

THE MONKEY

The fifty-year-old novel that launched Roth into fame and infamy, *Portnoy's Complaint*, boasts an inventive structure and will make you laugh out loud. The entire text is composed of the main character, Alexander Portnoy, ranting, declaiming, whining, describing, kvetching, and indeed complaining to his analyst, Dr. Spielvogel. Our point of view as readers is completely focalized through Portnoy so that Roth never attempts to bring in the consciousness of the women characters. The diegetic chronology is out of joint with time, toggling back and forth between the hilarities of Portnoy's Jersey childhood and various other moments in college and beyond. Among Portnoy's many problems is that he lives "a life *without* latent content" (*Portnoy* 257, italics in original). Freud encourages us to see the latent content of dreams as the source of their deep significance: it is from "their *latent* content, or (as we say) the 'dream-thoughts' [. . .] that we disentangle its meaning" (311, italics in original). In other words, when Roth claims Portnoy has no latent content he means that Portnoy need not imagine, for example, a castrating mother because his mother actually threatens him with a knife and undresses in front of him (not at the same time). While Portnoy has no latent content, the text Roth writes does—and that latent content manifests forcefully when Roth casts Portnoy as the (female) victim in an inversion of "Leda and the Swan." The latent content of Roth's novel emerges in this scene in particular but also in many of the possible readings against the grain, or through the manifest content of the text.

An unmarried Assistant Commissioner for The City of New York Commission on Human Opportunity, Portnoy is a thirty-three-year-old who refuses to "settle down" and have children with a nice Jewish girl to please his caricatured parents, Jack and Sophie Portnoy; he prefers not to realize his great promise as the Einstein of Weequahic, New Jersey. Portnoy tells Dr. Spielvogel about liaisons with many women, but one of the most memorable is his relationship with Mary Jane Reed, dubbed "The Monkey" because of "a little perversion she once engaged in" (106). Portnoy's mother sets up the assumption that most women are dumb and Portnoy is super smart on the second page of the novel: Hannah (Portnoy's older sister) is "no genius" whereas Portnoy is "Albert Einstein the Second!" (4). Indeed, Roth begins the novel with "she was so deeply imbedded in my consciousness" (3) so we are told point-blank that anything Portnoy's mother says will always already have been internalized.

Here is how Roth pens the first meeting between Portnoy and The Monkey (which is not the first time the reader meets her). They are in the city, at Lexington and 52nd, she tries to hail a cab and, seeing her "perfect nectarine" of an ass, a terrified Portnoy comes up to her with a soft "hi." "What do *you* want?" she asks, dismissively. "To buy you a drink," Portnoy says. Her response is a smirk: "A real swinger," to which Portnoy replies, "To eat your pussy, baby, how's that?" Instead of calling the cops as Portnoy imagines she will, she says, "That's better," they hop into a cab together and the rest is history (*Portnoy* 157-58, italics in original). The Monkey is a woman who likes to fuck and likes to experiment and disavows the pretense of the dance of seduction where a "drink" is a mask for what Portnoy—and, importantly, what she—really wants. Once Portnoy names his desire, she consents immediately and with abandon.[2] As Stryker and Penny and others have noted, consent culture has the potential to be a cure to rape culture, because once women's desires are no longer stigmatized, once the ridiculous assumptions that linger around "nice girls" disappear, then the whole charade of the many confusions about chasing/being chased and "no" really meaning "yes" evaporate. In a utopian world, then, women can say yes, mean it, and not be rendered "whores." The Monkey gets to occupy the first space (saying yes) but not the second (Roth paints her as a whore).[3]

But, she also wants to get married. And of course Portnoy thinks this will not do.

The first time the reader meets The Monkey, out of the diegetic chronology of the novel, she and Portnoy scream at each other in Athens, she balances, poised to jump off the balcony of their charming hotel because Portnoy won't marry her, and he jets off to Israel to escape. These are some of the descriptors Roth employs: "strange, lanky, and very batty" (*Portnoy* 105), "not too very bright" (106), "Confused, heartbroken, and also out of her mind" (106), "sly bitch" (107), "The cunt!" (107). Quite a collection of adjectives! But for all this, The Monkey has a point about Portnoy: he cares more for social justice than he does for her. "You mean, miserable hard-on you, you care more about the niggers in Harlem that you don't even know, than you do about me, who's been sucking you off for a solid year!" (106).

For all Portnoy's self-confessed pussy chasing—"it seems to make no difference how much the poor bastard actually gets, for he is dreaming about tomorrow's pussy even while pumping away at today's!" (102)—what he really cares about is his position as Assistant Commissioner. Portnoy fights not for women's liberation but for the liberation of oppressed men, women, and children in Harlem. Along with being dumb, The Monkey is racist. Portnoy, then, can see, name, and fight against oppression when it is racialized but not when it is gendered, and he can choose to ignore and even transform The Monkey's racism.

We can imagine Drenka in *Sabbath's Theater* (1995) as the three-dimensional, fully realized version of The Monkey. Among the most amazing of Roth's creations, Drenka, fifty something and extremely adventurous sexually, has Sabbath drinking out of her hand. Imaginative and compelling and in possession of a rich inner life, she is both a loving mother and a sexual woman who controls her narrative; she is not thirty years younger than the hero nor is she two-dimensionally thin, like The Monkey. And like The Monkey, Drenka expresses consent and desire without shame. Here is how Roth describes Drenka almost thirty years after introducing The Monkey:

> Drenka was a dark, Italian-looking Croat from the Dalmatian coast, on the short side like Sabbath, a full, firmly made woman at the provocative edge of being just overweight, her shape, at her heaviest, reminiscent of those clay figurines molded circa 2000 B.C., fat little dolls with big breasts and big thighs unearthed all the way from Europe down to Asia Minor and worshipped under a dozen different names as the great mother of the gods. (*Sabbath* 375)[4]

As this description augurs, Drenka will have a much thicker past, inner life, dreams, ambitions, thoughts, and desires, than The Monkey ever gets. From the first, Roth makes her similar to Sabbath whereas the Monkey and Portnoy are immediately contrasted—he is an intellectual and she is dumb, named after an animal for a sexual act, and angry, vindictive, and self-debasing. But still, Drenka is no Einstein; Roth paints her more fully and with more love and compassion than he does any other woman character and yet she still falls on one side of the unfortunate divide between smart and sexy.

Roth has Portnoy attempt to bridge that divide by making the sexy Monkey smarter. Among the books he gives her in his imagined Professor Higgins-ish course, "Professor Portnoy's 'Humiliated Minorities: An Introduction'" (*Portnoy* 209), are W. E. B. Du Bois's *The Souls of Black Folk* and James Baldwin's *Notes of a Native Son*. (Unsurprisingly the list does not include, say, Betty Friedan's 1963 *The Feminine Mystique*). Portnoy tries to get The Monkey to see the shared oppression of the working class from which she stems (Virginian coal mining family) and the black and Puerto Rican people he fights to defend in his work—but Roth does not have him connect these modes of oppression with sexism. She refuses and perceives this knowledge and these texts as useless, preferring to continue her racist and antisemitic ways. In the back of a cab she tells Portnoy his "black Hebe eyes" are giving off "radiation poisoning" (210) because she is wearing almost nothing to go meet the Mayor of New York, and then when they arrive at Gracie Mansion the taxi driver, one Manny Shapiro, calls her a "Nazi bitch!" before burning rubber to escape (211).

As Portnoy wrestles with his choice to stay with The Monkey despite her dumbness and antisemitism, which his tutoring does not ameliorate, he tells Dr. Spielvogel that he had, in the past, tried to be content with "erudite girls [...] lively, intelligent, self-respecting [...] girls in whose company I did not feel abject or ashamed. [...] And they didn't work out, either!" (215). Portnoy thus confesses that, while The Monkey's lack of education grates, the smart women fail to please as well. Portnoy spends a Thanksgiving with one such college girlfriend, Kay Campbell, dubbed The Pumpkin because of her large butt (the butts seem to invite food metaphors—recall The Monkey's nectarine ass). This scene of a nervous Jewish boy going home with a non-Jewish woman resonates with Alvy and Annie's Easter trip to the goyische home of Annie's parents in Woody Allen's *Annie Hall* (1977)—the same anxieties at play, the same culture shock of the quiet ways of the non-Jewish family.[5] Portnoy wonders with some surprise if Kay was "smarter really than I am" (224-25). Ultimately Portnoy lets her go because she won't convert to Judaism after they get married—a marriage only planned due to a false alarm pregnancy. Since Portnoy exclusively dates non-Jewish women, it of course makes no manifest sense that he would leave The Pumpkin because of her failure to convert, and Portnoy tells us he relished his "first un-sullied thrill of sadism with a woman!" after breaking her "gentile heart" (232). The manifest reason is that Kay refuses to become Jewish but the latent reason may well have to do with this tinge of sadism.

During a weekend trip to Vermont and other fall color spots, Portnoy, who had been struggling with the *shande* of shtupping a shikse, starts to feel true tenderness for The Monkey. Continuing his attempts to make her more erudite, in a cozy hotel room, calling himself "Porte-noir" (191), he recites Yeats's "Leda and the Swan."[6] Portnoy aligns himself with black masculinity when he playfully dubs himself "Porte-noir." While it would be some eight months later in the chronology of the plot when The Monkey would explicitly rail against Portnoy's concern for black people in Harlem, her slurs occur before this moment within the plotting of the novel, so his self-moniker here could have been taken by the readers as a reference to his work as the Commissioner. He attempts to teach his consort about oppression by recommending Baldwin and Du Bois, and here he positions himself with black masculinity in another scene of edification.

In the process of reciting "Leda and the Swan," Portnoy manifests some regrets, notices and names his "insensitivity," and goes on to explain that "I am smart and you are dumb" (192). This, according to Portnoy, is the true meaning of his recital of this poem to The Monkey, who, at the conclusion of the performance says: "Feel. It made my pussy all wet." To which Portnoy replies, "Sweetheart! You understood the poem!" (194). A few beats later The Monkey rejoins, "Oh, eat my educated cunt!" (194). "Leda and the Swan" has encouraged her to express enthusiastic consent for the very thing that got her to liaise with Portnoy in the first place.

Roth reminds us of The Monkey's dumbness—her literary comprehension comes entirely through her "educated cunt" so the dichotomy between smart and sexy remains firmly intact here. She is only smart insofar as she absorbs the meaning of Yeats's poem somatically. I like to imagine a counterfactual (or rather counterfictional) Monkey as a hot literary critic who could read "Leda and the Swan" with her brain *and* her body. This alternative Monkey might say something like: "Wow, this poem depicting Zeus in the form of a human-sized swan is about power and desire and while I identify with Leda, I feel split between the heat generated by 'a shudder in the loins engenders there' or 'her thighs caressed' and the horror at the mother of Helen being raped by an oversized swan. It's almost as though Yeats were celebrating rape and it is screwed up that he makes the overpowering of Leda so sexy. But I am also seeing how Leda offers a sort of weak consent." The Monkey might then have gone on to connect this deeply troubling eroticizing of rape with

Portnoy's own self-confessed sadism. But Roth did not write her this way. He did, though, offer us a through-the-looking-glass moment by inverting the power and gender dynamics set up by Yeats.

The diegetic point during which we meet The Monkey, at the end of their star-crossed romance, is the same moment when Portnoy flees to Israel to escape her. In the promised land, Portnoy meets Naomi, an Israeli who reminds him forcefully of his mother. He invites the gritty soldier Naomi back to his hotel and there they enact scenes deeply resonant with "Leda and the Swan"—only Portnoy, despite using his cousin Heshie's weights year-round and admiring his own muscles, is no Zeus. When Portnoy tries to overpower her and rape her, "*Boom,* she jumped to her feet. Pity the Syrian terrorist who tried to take her by surprise!" (263, italics in original). Yeats's Leda is very much taken by surprise when the Swan suddenly grasps her; indeed, "Leda" begins with "A sudden blow; the great wings beating still / Above the staggering girl" (Yeats 81). Then a few lines later Portnoy tells us "I reached for a breast and with a sharp upward snap of the skull, she butted me on the underside of the jaw" (*Portnoy* 264). Here Roth neatly reverses Yeats's power dynamic so that whereas the Swan has Leda's "nape caught in his bill / He holds her helpless breast upon his breast" (Yeats 81), when Portnoy reaches for Naomi's breast, his neck becomes caught just as Leda's was trapped in the swan's bill. Then, as Portnoy continues to try to master her, he imagines telling Naomi to "unlock your fortressy thighs, open wide that messianic Jewish hole!" (*Portnoy* 268). This strongly resonates with Yeats's question: "How can those terrified vague fingers push / The feathered glory from her loosening thighs?" (Yeats 81). But Yeats has Leda's thighs "loosen" while Roth has Naomi's thighs remain "fortressy." Finally, Naomi kicks him with her "powerful leg" and Portnoy wonders whether it's "The blow I had been angling for?" (*Portnoy* 270), thus using verbatim Yeats's opening salvo.

By reversing the power dynamics in Yeats's poem, Roth has the character of Portnoy, as a "fallen, psychoneurotic Jewish" (268) man, reveal the vast difference between goyische masculinity and diasporic Jewish American masculinity that simply cannot take, and cannot rise to the occasion of, powerful Jewish women. Portnoy's putz turns to tapioca in Israel; he cannot get excited about a Jewish woman. Whereas he has no trouble sexually with the hot and dumb types like The Monkey, a smart, articulate, socialist Israeli soldier makes him wither. Roth has Portnoy attribute this impudence to "The Monkey's revenge" (271). Because he degraded her, she has magically prevented all future hard-ons: "YOU ARE JUSTLY SENTENCED TO A LIMP DICK. GO FIND ANOTHER WAY TO HURT A PERSON" (272). The all-caps indicate the Kafkaesque roar of Portnoy's imagined Judge and the hurt that could have come from the now elusive unlimp dick indicates rape and/or sexual debasement.

Roth had prefigured this turn to "Leda and the Swan" much earlier in the novel when, kvetching about smothering Jewish mothers, Portnoy invokes the "big smothering bird beating frantic wings about my face and mouth *so that I cannot even get my breath*" (121, italics in original). Naomi reminds him of his mother, further underscoring the power inversion between Yeats's poem and Roth's recasting.

Roth has Portnoy fully recognize that there is something "wrong" with his inability to attach to a woman who is smart, sexy, and self-assured, but at the close of the novel Portnoy remains firmly mired in this dilemma and unable to resolve his issues. The parade of male characters who follow him include: Peter Tarnopol with his caustic, lying, cheating wife Maureen (*My Life as a Man* [1970]); "Philip Roth" with the antisemitic Jinx (*Operation Shylock* [1993]); Swede Levov (*American Pastoral* [1997]) with his face-lifted beauty queen wife; Coleman Silk (*The Human Stain* [2000]) with his illiterate, debased, thirty-years-younger mistress; Simon Axler (*The Humbling* [2009]) with his young, lesbian lover Pegeen, ripe to make over *Pretty Woman* style, and on and on. None of these male characters seems to have learned much over the years. They are stuck in Portnoy's dilemma and they all have problems attaching to smart and sexy and self-assured women who offer consent without shame. In this way Roth demonstrates some of the major problems with these varieties of masculinity; by not resolving Portnoy's dilemma, by continuing to craft men who struggle with the same divide, Roth indicates that not much has changed despite some outward manifestations of gender equity.

Whereas Portnoy explains that The Monkey has a very low opinion of herself and a very high opinion of him, Vivian Gornick finds that Jewish writers such as Roth and Bellow have a low opinion of themselves and they therefore take to "savaging" women in order to boost their egos. Gornick argues in an interview that, "Roth and Bellow suffer from feeling like such outsiders in gentile culture that savaging women seems justified. So in that sense there's a connection between Jewishness and misogyny. I don't think Jews are more misogynistic than gentiles. We're talking about these writers." Gornick here suggests that the sadism to which Portnoy confesses stems from being cast out of gentile culture. To me it seems rather that Roth dramatizes Portnoy's dilemma in ways that illuminate at least some of the problematic expectations of masculine culture and its desires. Clearly, much more work on Roth and gender needs to be done.

An excellent collection of articles on Roth and Women is to be found in the *Philip Roth Studies* special issue with that name. In the introduction, David

Gooblar invites a promising scholar to write the definitive monograph on "Roth and Women." It's amazing it hasn't happened yet and I hope it does. While a monograph does not yet exist, there are many superb and sensitive articles and essays in journals and collections on Roth that nuance his take on gender. Some critics have found that Roth's focus on masculinity in effect exposes rather than endorses misogyny.[7] "Roth's work," argues Debra Shostak, "can appear as much a prescient critique of misogynist attitudes as a purveyor of them" (112). I agree completely and have tried to stay true to this nuanced reading here. Shortly after Roth's death, Mike Witcombe wrote an article in *The Conversation* entitled "Was Philip Roth a Misogynist?"[8] Witcombe reviews many of the critiques leveled at Roth and charts some of the changes so this provides a rich resource for further exploration. Some critics have even found Roth to be a feminist.[9] I definitely would not go that far. But I do think, in celebrating the superlative prose, in reading closely for the counter-narratives, in laughing along with and *at* Portnoy, in trying to reclaim and imagine a mix of sexy *and* smart for some of the women in Roth's novels, in finding some power in Roth's portrait of women who offer consent without shame, we can reinvigorate the lost joys of hilarious, zany novels like *Portnoy's Complaint*.

PUNCH LINE

One. And it isn't funny.

(Or is it?)

ENDNOTES

1. I am very grateful to Justine Murison for suggesting Penny's article and Roupenian's short story in the context of this essay and to Lilya Kaganovsky for telling me the joke that became my title; I am enormously thankful to both and to Anke Pinkert for their invaluable feedback on this piece.

2. For more on consent culture see Stryker.

3. See Roupenian and also Grady's article about all the brouhaha "Cat-Person" caused on the question of consent, desire, and saying no after saying yes.

4. Alex Hobbs finds that, "Drenka is a complex character, who embraces her sexual identity. In a play on her name, she is, perhaps, drunk on the power of her sexual identity and the sheer amount of men she can attract; she certainly relishes the feeling of euphoria that successful conquests give her" (87).

5. See Girgus.

6. The Monkey is not the only racist woman in Roth's oeuvre—Delphine Roux, from *The Human Stain* (2000), is an anti-sex, anti-pleasure, secretly racist scholar of French literature and theory. Roux is smart, but definitely not sexy. *Operation Shylock's* Jinx, on the other hand, "really got into hating Jews when [she] was a Christian" (210)—a former antisemite, Jinx is sexy, not smart. For more on race in Roth see Franco; Kaplan.

7. See Ivanova.

8. Carmen Calil, founder of the Feminist Press, Virago, resigned from the Man Booker Prize committee because she found Roth's work self-centered and repetitive. Although she explicitly resigned because she found it bad writing, the general assumption was that she walked away in protest of his misogyny. Instead, she explains, "I'd no idea—and I'm nearly 73 for goodness sake—I had no idea that his work was objected to because he is seen as a misogynist" (cited in Flood).

9. Marshall Bruce Gentry finds in reference to *American Pastoral* that "Roth has written a feminist novel" (163) but he argues this somewhat circuitously by claiming that, "Roth's females here are products of a deeply American misogyny that are desperate to battle and from which Roth is distancing himself" (165).

WORKS CITED

Flood, Alison. "Philip Roth Protest had Nothing to do with Feminism, Says Virago Founder," *Guardian*, 21 May 2011. https://www.theguardian.com/books/2011/may/21/philip-roth-protest-feminism-virago.

Franco, Dean. *Race, Rights, and Recognition: Jewish American Literature Since 1969*. Cornell UP, 2012.

Freud, Sigmund. *The Interpretation of Dreams*, 1900, translated by James Strachey, Avon Books, 1965.

Gentry, Bruce Marshall. "Newark Maid Feminism in Philip Roth's *American Pastoral*." *Turning up the Flame: Philip Roth's Later Novels*, edited by Jay Halio and Ben Siegel, U of Delaware P, 2005, pp. 160-71.

Girgus, Sam B. "Philip Roth and Woody Allen: Freud and the Humor of the Repressed." *Semites and Stereotypes: Characteristics of Jewish Humor*, edited by Avner Ziv and Anat Zajdman, Greenwood, 1993, pp. 121-30.

Gornick, Vivian. "Demon Doubt." An interview with Rebecca Tuhus-Dubrow, *Boston Review*, 5 August 2008. http://bostonreview.net/books-ideas/vivian-gornick-men-my-life-interview.

Grady, Constance. "The Uproar over the New Yorker Short Story 'Cat Person' Explained," *Vox*, 12 December 2017. https://www.vox.com/culture/2017/12/12/16762062/cat-person-explained-new-yorker-kristen-roupenian-short-story.

Hobbs, Alex. "What Women Want Is Actually What Men Want Too: Yearning for Connection in Philip Roth's *Sabbath's Theater*." *Critique: Studies in Contemporary Fiction*, vol. 54, no. 1, 2013, pp. 81-95.

Ivanova, Velichka. "My Own Foe from the Other Gender: (Mis)representing Women in *The Dying Animal*." *Philip Roth Studies*, vol. 8 no. 1, 2012, pp. 31-44.

Kaplan, Brett Ashley. *Jewish Anxiety and the Novels of Philip Roth*. Bloomsbury, 2015.

Penny, Laurie. "The Horizon of Desire," *Longreads*, October 2017. https://longreads.com/2017/10/10/the-horizon-of-desire/.

Roth, Philip. *Operation Shylock*. 1993. The Library of America, 2010.

---. *Portnoy's Complaint*. New York: Vintage Books, 1969.

---. *Sabbath's Theater*. 1995. The Library of America, 2010.

Roupenian, Kirsten. "Cat-Person," *New Yorker*, 11 December 2017, https://www.newyorker.com/magazine/2017/12/11/cat-person.

Shostak, Debra. "Roth and Gender." *The Cambridge Companion to Philip Roth,* edited by Timothy Parrish, Cambridge, UP, 2007, pp. 111-26.

Stryker, Kitty. *Ask: Building Consent Culture.* Portland: Thorntree Press, 2017.

Witcombe, Mike. "Was Philip Roth a Misogynist?" *The Conversation,* 23 May 2018, https://theconversation.com/was-philip-roth-a-misogynist-97114

Yeats, William Butler. "Leda and the Swan." *W. B. Yeats: Selected Poems,* selected by John Kelly. London: Phoenix Poetry, 2002.

Newark Revisited

A Philip Roth for the
Twenty-First Century

Michael Kimmage

Philip Roth died in the second year of the Trump presidency. He was a critic of the new president in sharper terms than he had been of George W. Bush or even Richard Nixon, whose shadow falls across a number of Roth's novels. Apart from Roth's opposition to the Vietnam War, to which he devoted a small portion of his literary celebrity—his name, as it were—Roth was never an overtly political writer or an overtly political man. He was an FDR Democrat, and in this he was his father's son. That made him, as he surely knew, somewhat uninteresting as an American writer. It would have been interesting if he had, like John Updike, come out in favor of the Vietnam War. It would have been interesting if he had been a Marxist or a Zionist or a neoconservative. There is no political destiny for an American writer less gripping intellectually and culturally than to be centrist Democrat. For this reason, Roth had a political profile that almost erased itself. As times goes by, his boring political profile is likely to be erased from the memory of his life and career.

As Roth himself would have been the first to argue, he should be remembered for his literature, for his many books, and not for the political positions he took in public or in private. Yet it would be a mistake to place politics on one side of Roth's critical reception and literature on the other. It would be an even worse mistake to do so in the wake of the Trump presidency, which has altered the texture of American politics and which has issued from an alteration in the texture of American politics. To these alterations Roth's literature has much to say. Events can occasion the rediscovery or rethinking of an existing body of literature—the Nixon presidency, for example, that made Roth think he was living in Kafka's America (see his 1974 essay "Our Castle"); or the reappearance of *Moby-Dick* in the 1930s after decades of callous neglect, just in time for Captain Ahab to accompany the fascist dictators leading their respective *Pequods* into the abyss. *The Plot Against America* has proven itself a major novel of the Trump era, from which it will be forever inseparable as gloss and as prophecy, despite having been published in 2004. At least as rich is Roth's so-called American Trilogy and through it his literature of place, of de-industrialization, of American decay—in a word, his literature of Newark, New Jersey. This was the anti-celebratory fiction Roth fashioned in a decade far more hospitable to self-celebration. Finally, Roth's sense of himself as a civic writer and his sense of his novels as civic in nature and effect bears directly on the fractures and divisions of the Trump era. Roth's books are a meditation on a nation's story conceived in the glow of World War II patriotism and carried a bit beyond the end of the twentieth century. This meditation is frozen in time. It ceased with Roth's death in May 2018, but because it took shape in literature and is alive with the life of its readers, Roth's meditation is also ongoing. It evolves every time his books are read in real time.

***

Upon publication, *The Plot Against America* was misread as an exposé of the Bush administration. The misreading assumed it to be a *roman à clef* in which the Charles Lindbergh who assumes the presidency in place of Franklin Roosevelt represented George W. Bush. Indeed, this could only have been a misreading of Roth's counter-factual novel. Charles Lindbergh was famously an isolationist. He was an anti-Semite, a harsh opponent of FDR, and an American who was partial to the National Socialists in Germany, who in turn regarded him as the beau ideal of the Aryan hero. (Hermann Goering owed his ascent within the Nazi movement to his celebrity status as a World War I pilot.) The historical Lindbergh and the one who surfaces in *The Plot Against America* is a foe of the constitutional order. As the novel's plot reveals, he is in fact a German plant within the American system—that is the plot against America. George W. Bush was something else entirely. He was the inverse of an isolationist. He was no anti-Semite. He did not define himself by hatred toward the Democratic Party, and the ideological thread of his presidency was a loathing of authoritarianism. President Bush's errors in Iraq stemmed from his ideal of liberty, the sweeping program of ending tyranny in our time that he articulated in his Second Inaugural Address (delivered not long after *The Plot Against America* was published). Bush's were not the errors of a latter-day Lindbergh.

The Trump presidency, by contrast, fits the pattern of this 2004 novel far better. Roth's novel is an essay on irrationalism in politics and an essay on fear. The population—terrified by the prospect of its own undoing, terrified by the course of events—succumbs to a dictator's serpentine promises. The fear is the precondition. The dictator then uses subterfuge to build upon this fear, singling out enemies but doing so in way that is both visible and veiled. The nightmare unfolds step by step. President Lindbergh's agenda is not to disestablish Jewish life through open violence, not at first. It is to make the Jews of the United States morally invisible and in the dark spaces of their invisibility to work toward their eventual exclusion from the body politic. Left offstage in *The Plot Against America* is the possible physical annihilation of the Jews. Lindbergh is deposed before that can happen; but the path from normalcy to catastrophe is laid out with enough precision for the catastrophe to be thinkable. Indeed, that is the novel's whole point as literature: to puncture complacency and to explore the contours of normalcy by making the unthinkable thinkable. The Trump administration is not tending toward a Holocaust. The elements Roth assembled in *The Plot Against America*, however, are all in evidence: the marriage of fear and irrationalism, the subterfuge of lies and conspiratorial reasoning and the application of moral invisibility to a shifting set of groups—Muslims, immigrants, the transgendered and so on. The descent of political civility into barbarism, presented with a cartographer's attention to detail in the *Plot Against America*, is arrestingly familiar to readers of the novel who have been experiencing the Trump era in real time.

All of this has been noticed by the novel's most recent readers. There is yet another remarkable concordance that has been less remarked upon. In *The Plot Against America*, Lindbergh's presidency is the function of German espionage. When this becomes clear, Lindbergh literally vanishes into thin air. The plot, having been unraveled, unravels. This particular plot corresponds strangely to the story of Russian meddling in the 2016 election. Lindbergh's fawning before Hitler parallels Trump's fawning before Putin in his speeches, in conversation, and when the two heads of state met in Helsinki in the summer of 2018. Amusingly, the issue of Russian meddling in 2016 is often described as having been inconceivable, unimaginable, unfathomable, and yet it had been imagined in the pages of a novel published twelve years before the meddling took place. Regardless of whether the novel and the Mueller report line up, the truest concordance between fact and fiction is that of mood. Roth wonderfully anticipated the disorientation of American politics after 2016, the disruption of norms and conventions and constitutional procedures that had been so blandly effective up to that point that they had hardly been noticed in daily life. Then, because of the plot, they are upended. The slender thread of normalcy and predictability snaps, and the United States finds itself much as Europe did in the summer of 1914 or the autumn of 1939, aware only that a pillar of stability is no longer there and unsure of how to regain the status quo ante. On this point the 2004 novel and the events of 2017 and 2018 run together.

Circa 2018 the American Trilogy offers a different kind of guidance to the perplexed. Published between 1997 and 2000, it came at the conclusion of an immensely successful decade for the United States. The decade began with the end of the Cold War. It witnessed the massive growth of the American economy, multiple technological revolutions, and expansive foreign-policy influence. Two cities captured the upward trajectory. One was Rudy Giuliani's New York City, which appeared to vanquish crime and to be amassing unspeakable wealth at the same time. *Sex and the City*, a popular TV show of the period, presented Manhattan as a metropolis of uninterruptable pleasure and wealth: it was the decade's credible fantasy. San Francisco was the other urban star of the 1990s, demonstrating the rewards entrepreneurs skilled in the arts of disruption were destined to enjoy. The decade's typical worry was about excess, about going too far too quickly, damaging the environment perhaps in the process and damaging one's spiritual integrity—the sins of growth, motion, power, privilege, decadence, overreach.

In the midst of the national party, Roth wrote the American Trilogy. They were books with range. There was lots of New England in them. They end with a depopulated United States, the European settlement of the continent wiped away, leaving boulders and mountains and the water turning endlessly over itself in the final paragraph of *The Human Stain*. The Trilogy's three novels travel frequently to New York City, to the bohemian streets of Greenwich Village, to the city's radical underground and its monied townhouses. But where these novels reside is in Newark. Newark is everywhere in them, the houses and streets, the ethnic enclaves, the professions listed and observed, recorded and filed away into the vast archive of Philip Roth's oeuvre. Newark is where everything begins. It is the child's city perceived without guile, without knowledge, without memory, and still more it is the remembered city, the city of the adult who is no longer there, who left intending never to set foot in the unremarkable provinces again, to take the remarkable metropole by storm, and who cannot forget the ancestral home. It is the city to which the Swede must return in *American Pastoral* even when he has moved out and moved his business out, because it is the city in which he grew up, the city he cannot escape. His daughter chooses to die in Newark, the prison house of memory, the unwanted anchor on American individualism, and at the same time the Garden of Eden. Newark is the startling repository of American innocence before it is paradise lost, which is the last thing those not from Newark might ascribe to this prosaic industrial city at the foot of New York City.

Existential Newark, the Newark that shapes the American Trilogy's characters, is secondary to the city itself, and the actual city is the city that fails.

Worst of all for Newark, it fails while the country around it is flourishing. Of course Philip Roth was from Newark. The city chose him more than he chose it as his great literary subject, but once Newark had chosen him by accident Roth turned the accident into an inevitability. Newark is a seventeenth-century American city. It had its role to play in the American Revolution and Civil War. It was an industrial behemoth of the late nineteenth century and hence a magnet for immigrants. These immigrants from Europe and in a different sense from the American South built up the mid-century metropolis of Roth's youth. That was the heroic trajectory, from colonial times to triumph in the Second World War. Newark was as indelibly an arsenal of democracy in the 1940s as any other American place. And then came the cataclysm—the flight of the middle-class white populations, the steady collapse of the industrial economy, the racial animosities, the declining tax base, the abandonment of the city, the crime and the riots. The city's failure allows Roth to chart evolutions in his Newark-born characters in the American trilogy, but it also allows Roth to tell an unexpected story about the American nation, which is not precisely a story about the failure of places like Newark and not precisely a story about the postwar validations of American life (post-World War II and perhaps even more post-Cold War). It is the story of mutual incomprehension: the triumphant nation that cannot explain the disaster of Newark; the relegation of Newark to a punch line rather than to a place that makes American sense; and the embattled city condemned to look across the water to resplendent, indifferent Manhattan. *All right we are two countries.* So runs a famous line from John Dos Passos's *U.S.A.* trilogy, but that was a trilogy written and set in the Great Depression. These two countries were more radically divided in the 1990s, in the second gilded age, than in the decade when the stock market's crash pulled an entire nation down to earth. All right we are two countries was the lesson encoded in Roth's home town.

We are two countries was no less the campaign slogan of candidate Trump. His chosen backdrop on the campaign trail was cities much like Newark, though his identification was not with the African American and minority communities of these cities but with the white working class and aggrieved middle class on their peripheries. His identification, curiously enough, was with the failure of these places, the symbolic failure of the industrial economy, of the Clevelands, the Buffalos, the Detroits poured into a single word in Trump's inaugural address—carnage. He associated himself with the carnage as no other American presidential candidate had ever done, and this was not because he had read Roth's American Trilogy. Had he read these books, he would not have sympathized with the politics of their author, which would be difficult at any rate to discern from the novels themselves; and by no means was Roth writing these books in hopes that a wealthy man's son from Queens might ride the motif of American carnage to the White House. But this much adds up: after the financial crisis of 2008, the failure of Newark Roth describes in the American Trilogy was more palpable to the American electorate than it had been in the 1990s.

If back then Newark was a place on the margins, by 2016 New York City (where Hillary Clinton headquartered her campaign) and San Francisco were ripe for political marginalization. They were too obscenely rich and successful to represent the country at large. The problem perhaps was that too few Democrats had read the American Trilogy and taken it to heart. They recognized the anger within the two nations, the anger that there were two nations, only when it was too late. They missed the Homeric rage Roth sang in these lines (from *American Pastoral*) about the Newark riots: "Yes, here it is, let it come, yes, the magnificent opportunity, one of human history's rare transmogrifying moments: the old ways of suffering are burning blessedly away in the flames, never again to be resurrected, instead to be superseded, within only hours, by suffering that will be so gruesome, so monstrous, so unrelenting and abundant, that its abatement will take the next five hundred years" (*Pastoral* 268). Rage and suffering as the parameters of an American moment, an American era: it was a libretto inaudible to the Democratic Party in 2016, though it was not silent or undiscoverable. It happened to be the very libretto of the winning candidate.

***

Philip Roth is no longer with us. He was an old man when he died, and the workings of sexuality and gender in his novels will not endear him to the contemporary reader. His priestly devotion to literature is a more and more uncommon quality in American culture, as Roth insistently pointed out in his non-fiction writings, predicting that the novel would go the way of Latin poetry in a decade or two. On this Roth may not have been wrong. In addition, his genius was his own. It will never be replicated. Yet the novels will create their own readership. They will not depend on academics or critics. Since *Goodbye, Columbus* they have never suffered for readers, and they will make their claim on this readership as they always have, living novels of the future just as they were once the living novels of the 1960s or the 1990s.

When they make their claim, they will illustrate a literary endeavor that was not of the Democratic Party and that was neither liberal nor conservative. Roth's was a civic literary endeavor, one that grew from his enjoyment of relating the Jewish-American narrative into his enjoyment of relating the American narrative or deconstructing the American narrative or unearthing a counter-factual American narrative. Cosmopolitan that Roth was, in his novels citizen writer wrote for citizen reader, never preaching to the choir—more often needling the reader, prodding the reader into certain kinds of discomfort, confusion, indignation and, along the way, into certain kinds of insight. The goal was a citizen with imagination. As the United States finds itself in civic crisis, Roth can be turned to not just as a superb writer but as a necessary writer. Roth's novels are with us, intact, thank God. They are a bridge for the citizen to walk, a bridge from fear and into the open plains of the imagination, from the fear of having a nemesis to the remembered courage Bucky Cantor the javelin thrower demonstrates in the last paragraph of Roth's last work of fiction, *Nemesis*, a javelin thrower who no doubt represented the truest intentions of the author himself.

WORK CITED

Roth, Philip. *American Pastoral*. Houghton, 1997.

ARTICLE

Philip Roth in His Silence

Pia Masiero

I had the chance to meet Philip Roth in person just once, during the celebration of his eightieth birthday in Newark, back in 2013. I was invited among many other members of the Philip Roth Society and my meeting the man actually amounted to shaking his hand and sharing a couple of thoughts, including my invitation (declined) to come to the Venice International Literary Festival I direct. On that occasion, he spoke to the gathering about the motivations for his decision to stop writing fiction. The news had already got out, but hearing it in his own voice made it more authentically final. He told us: "I don't want to describe the blade of the auger that you use for ice-fishing [...]. I don't want to describe, spadeful by spadeful, how a grave is dug [...]. I don't want to describe another death [...]. I don't wish any longer to contemplate in fiction the destructive, the blighted, the bruised, the assailable, the accused, their accusers, or even those who are whole, sane, and beautifully intact" ("The Ruthless Intimacy of Fiction" 394).

We officially entered a new phase then—the phase of his fictional silence. Silence is certainly close to death—one might venture to say it prefigures it—but it is not death: Roth could still—if sparingly—be interviewed, he could still be met near his Upper West Side New York apartment: fictionally silent, yes, but alive. Most of all, during his birthday at the Newark library he presented the decision to stop writing fiction as joyful: "I for one awoke one fine morning with a smile on my face, understanding that miraculously, seemingly in my sleep, I had at long last eluded my lifelong master: the stringent exigencies of literature" (393). How could we not connect—at least partially and in spite of our eagerness to have more to read and enjoy—with his smile and his sense of liberation? With Philip Roth's death, the prefiguration of death contained in his fictional silence has become the stark reality we have to face and accept—death's absolute silence.

The Italian philosopher Virgilio Melchiorre's words come to mind: "the other's absolute silence reveals that, from now on, a number of my possibilities have become impossibilities; specifically those possibilities, those modes of being, that I shared with the other [...]" (113, my transl.). He continues "[t]hose modes which are now impossible, those co-possibilities I cannot live with anyone else and which will be forever forbidden, are such because they are rooted in the other's existence [...]; that very life by which I was crossed, will never be given back to me" (114, my translation). We can easily relate to these words thinking about a beloved one with whom we shared moments and places, tears and laughter; and yet, when I think about it, Melchiorre's words would seem to apply to the case of Philip Roth as well, someone whom I have met vicariously, that is, through his books and on that single occasion in person. I believe this feeling is shared by many of his readers. Has this got to do with the way in which Roth writes or the way in which we read?

Let me try to answer this question starting from my own experience as a Roth reader. I did not arrive at Roth's books via the usual venues—his fellow Jewish American writers and his ambivalent relationship with his Jewish community—but through a syllabus meant to be read by a group of scholars variously (and loosely) related to American Studies, who came from eighteen countries. We spent six weeks together in Louisville attending the United States Department of State 2005 Institute on Contemporary Literature. To give you an idea of the diversity of the group, suffice it to say that I was the only one from the European Union. The book by Roth on the syllabus was *The Human Stain* and it joined a list comprising, among others, DeLillo, Gómez Peña, Pynchon, and Kingston. Sensibly enough, the book was intended to represent Jewish American writers, and a poetics apparently unaffected by postmodernism. To me, the book unleashed an infatuation for a master of narrative form well beyond the themes he presented to portray what it meant to be an American across racial and religious boundaries during "the piety binge, a purity binge" (*Stain*, in *Trilogy* 706) of the Clinton era. The complex narrative construction of *The Human Stain* presented to me a man in love with writing that perfectly suited a woman—me—who ever since grammar school has interpreted books as depending on formal choices for the magical effects they have on readers.

Retrospectively, I am more and more convinced that it was Nathan Zuckerman that did the trick. At the center of the book, there lies a writer who begins to write to make sense of a man he thought he knew but whose death turned out to be a mystery—"How did such a man as Coleman come to exist? What is it that he was?" (*Stain*, in *Trilogy* 1012). As with Seymour, the Swede, Levov, Nathan learns from a close relative of the deceased what actually occupied the existential center of his life: African American Coleman Silk interpreted the foundational American tenet of pioneering in terms of self-invention and passed for Jew. To ponder the complexity and depth of the friend who had danced him back to life and who had now become a mystery, Zuckerman does what he usually does when he needs to understand: he writes a book.

The seminal moment is worth quoting: "and not quite knowing what was happening, standing in the falling darkness beside the uneven earth mound roughly heaped over Coleman's coffin, I was completely seized by his story, by its end and by its beginning, and, then and there, I began this book" (1016). It is impossible not to see Philip Roth, the writer we are now mourning, in Zuckerman's response; it is much more than the myriad biographical overlappings between the two, especially in view of how Roth describes what happens to facts when "the butcher, imagination" (Searles 220) takes over. It is the unshakable belief that writing is quintessentially human as it contains the all-too human need to order the unordered reality that surrounds us to make sense of it. This belief is not rooted in an arrogant presumption of finding the truth with the capital letter—who does not remember and deeply relate to the magnificent if helplessly sad lines on being wrong again and again and again in *American Pastoral*?—but revolves around an attempt at approaching it that savors both of obsession and of devotion.

In Roth's hands "the stringent exigencies of literature" have touched all "the hypnotic materiality of the world" ("The Ruthless Intimacy of Fiction" 393) he lived in, macroscopically embracing American history in its defining twentieth-century moments and microscopically detailing "a butcher shop chicken or a gold-star flag" (393) in a mixture of "expansive engagement" and "fascination"; his "passion for local specificity" has always been his privileged way of touching the core of the tragedy and comedy that make us recognizably human. In the fictional building of the American Trilogy, which is structured around the same basic blueprint, we are given Roth's way of being in the world: Zuckerman learns something about a friend that reveals a depth that he had not fathomed, tries to find all the factual data he can get his hands on and then writes a book that makes narrative sense of those facts. Making narratively tenable choices is not simply honoring novelistic rules, but, much more relevantly, reconstructing the existential uniqueness of his exceptional friends and their emotional timbre. It is definitely an instance, to use the term Debra Shostak employs in reference to *The Counterlife*, of a "speculative narrative" ("This Obsessive" 198), but the speculation is anchored in an act of empathetic immersion and profound listening.

The Zuckerman of the American Trilogy is a mature writer who is aware that handling his materials is becoming more and more difficult and requires mobilizing all sorts of tools and attitudes to counter, diffuse, and negotiate what he knows. Interestingly, knowledge is not presented as something that helps the writer, but as something that complicates the handling of his materials. And yet Roth (via Zuckerman) is clear in indicating knowledge and understanding as the outcomes of the narrative managing of his materials.

Thus, paradoxically, knowing is both a hindrance and an objective. In one of the moments in which Zuckerman's voice becomes audible from within the claustrophobic folds of the Swede's desperate interior probing, we come across the repetition of this basic tenet, which is all the more significant given its unexpected positioning: "[h]ow he managed to get to [Hamlin's widow's] house for tea is another story—another *book*—but he did it" (*Pastoral*, in *Trilogy* 201, italics in original).

The three distinct narrative choices that constitute the narrative skeleton of the three books that make up the American Trilogy demonstrate how novelistic form has to be interpreted as organically emerging from the raw materials the writer is confronted with. The Swede's unrelentingly limited perspective in *American Pastoral* emerging within the folds of an imagined realistic chronicle, the dialogic invisibility of the author in *I Married a Communist*, the authorially controlled, multivoiced perspectives in *The Human Stain*, are the narratological outcomes of Roth's finding (via Zuckerman) the shape for the telling of his protagonists' stories that is best suited to the purpose of getting them across to the reader.

In Livia Manera's last interview with Philip Roth, he answers her question "What did you gain in becoming a more mature writer?" in this way: "I gained maturity, which for me, as a novelist, meant an awareness of the deeper dimensions of the novel itself. I discovered that the power of the novel lies in the richness of the mixture of its parts. Or perhaps what I discovered were riches within me that only the passage of time—the years and years of writing and living—could make accessible." And he adds: "Instead of becoming easier, with the growth and maturity of one's talent, the struggle with one's material expands—or that at least has been my experience. The more I knew, the harder it got."[1] Zuckerman's struggling with his materials is a transversal theme in the trilogy and is a narrative thread that is explicitly presented at least in *The Human Stain* and in *American Pastoral*. We are told about the Swede and Coleman Silk and about the way in which Zuckerman has handled his materials—gradually in the final installment of the trilogy and almost as a transcendental visitation in the first, during the dance with Joy ("I began gazing into his life [. . .] and *inexplicably*, which is to say lo and behold, I found him in Deal, New Jersey" [*Pastoral*, in *Trilogy* 85, emphasis mine]). Zuckerman, deep in the ventriloquist act that constitutes him, presents fictionally what Roth is talking about when he speaks of the mature writer. For both of them, "the more I knew, the harder it got": it does not become easier to make sense of life as you grow older, and consequently writing becomes more challenging. Playing the role he attributes to himself in *I Married a Communist*, the mere listener who passively receives the stories someone decides to narrate, is a subtle way to reflect on the role of the reader who finds himself/herself rhetorically manipulated by the narrator.

When *Exit Ghost* made clear that Roth was done with Zuckerman for good, fictionally presenting him as a writer who could not do what he had been doing all his life essentially because he no longer had the kind of memory that novelistic writing required, we mourned him not only as individual readers, but as a scholarly community, as the Fall 2009 special issue of Philip Roth Studies titled "Mourning Zuckerman" testifies. We mourned Nathan Zuckerman both as readers and scholars not simply because Zuckerman had been with us for over thirty years and we had experienced his struggles, dreams and predicaments as those of a fellow being, thanks to a sufficiently coherent "continuing consciousness" (Palmer 15) that we could recognize over nine books, but also because he stands for what we were through those thirty years.

Let me explain this more precisely, as this will lead us back to my initial question. Reading happens in our lives as an embodied experience which is uniquely specific to the moment in time we do it. Books and the characters that inhabit them bear the traces of our own lives. They become repositories of bits and pieces of our former selves and hold the promise of reminding us of our emotional and existential bearings in a given time and place. It may be argued that Roth cannot be reduced to Nathan Zuckerman and his books. That is obviously true, but I think there is no disputing that the cornerstone in the construction of "Philip Roth" is his being a self-conscious (Jewish) writer steeped in the evolving history of American society in the final decades of the twentieth century. This is why I have employed an autobiographical slant— my own entering into Philip Roth's story-worlds via Zuckerman and his own fictional death—as my formal choice to organically address the silence we are now surrounded by.

Philip Roth's death constitutes a loss also because my possibilities as a reader rooted in his existence as a writer have become an impossibility. The traces of me that his books preserve are still there but belong only in a past-oriented file that cannot but become more and more difficult to open with the passing of time. The silence of death has shut for us the possibility of a future-oriented encounter with ourselves in the unique way in which Roth's books triggered it. "I am no longer many things I once was and no longer able to do any number of things I once did. At eighty-four, giving things up is a way of life. What I do not have, I live without" (Manera). We too cannot but accept what we do not have and what we must live without—learning once again from him an acceptance that is a profound act of responsibility.

NOTE

1. The interview was published in Italian. I thank Livia Manera, who e-mailed me the text of Philip Roth's original answers.

WORKS CITED

Manera, Livia. "Ecco perché ho smesso di scrivere." *laLettura* #301, 3 September 2017.

Melchiorre, Virgilio. *Al di là dell'ultimo. Filosofie della morte e filosofie della vita.* Vita e Pensiero, 1998.

Palmer, Alan. *Fictional Minds.* U of Nebraska P, 2004.

Roth, Philip. *The American Trilogy.* The Library of America, 2011.

---. "The Ruthless Intimacy of Fiction." *Why Write? Collected Nonfiction 1960-2013.* The Library of America, pp. 391-404.

Searles, George J., editor. *Conversations with Philip Roth.* UP of Mississippi, 1992.

Shostak, Debra. "'This Obsessive Reinvention of the Real': Speculative Narrative in Philip Roth's *The Counterlife.*" *Modern Fiction Studies,* vol. 37, no. 2, 1991, pp. 197-215.

ARTICLE

Testosterone and Sympathy

Maggie McKinley

I recall a moment in graduate school when I was sitting in the library, reading *Portnoy's Complaint*. A fellow graduate student walked by and said to me, "You know, I just can't read Philip Roth. Too testosterone-y." Her tone was good-natured, the comment merely a flippant observation, likely meant to invite a laugh (I obliged). Such a remark might sound familiar to anyone, anywhere who has ever studied Roth, taught Roth, read Roth in a public place, idly picked up a Roth novel in a bookstore, or thought enough about Roth that someone nearby could *just tell*. The testosterone!

At that nascent moment of my academic career—a point at which I hadn't yet read much Roth, nor much *about* Roth—such an offhanded comment was not as familiar as it would become, so the remark caught me somewhat off guard. That might seem naïve or disingenuous, considering *Portnoy's* subject matter (it's only page 17, after all, when we confront "WHACKING OFF"), but I was not well versed in the various modes of anger and discomfort Roth's writing had inspired for decades. Thus, I had no witticism to toss back in reply, no prepared counter-argument for all of Roth's merits as a writer, no concise one-liner that would leave any casual Roth skeptic speechless. (To be honest, I still don't really have this). Though I brushed off the exchange and didn't think that I cared much, it clearly had some impact on me, as it's occupied a place in my mind for years; I vividly remember that passing comment from over a decade ago, while I've forgotten many more important things I likely should have retained from graduate school.

That remark or something like it has since been repeated to me count-less times, in various ways. There was the dissertation committee member who asked, in response to my project on Roth, Mailer, Bellow, Baldwin, and Wright: "How can you spend so much time with all these *men?*" There is the recurrent response to my research from friends and colleagues: "Huh. Why *Roth?*"—a loaded question that can be interpreted as either genuine curiosity, polite skepticism, or thinly veiled judgment, depending on the delivery. Regardless of context, these situations force me into a position of defense, and I often feel as though they function as some kind of test: I must say the right thing *or else!* I'll lose the audience! They'll walk away confirmed in their notion that Philip Roth is, in fact, too testosterone-y!

The issue is, of course, that Roth's work *does* feature its share of testosterone. I am not here to deny that the protagonist of all but one of Roth's books is male, or that the central themes of most of his work center on definitions, defenses, and anxieties related to masculinity, specifically virility and potency. "Bless me with manhood!" Alex Portnoy cries (37), shortly after describing the evening that he cored an apple and promptly "ran off into the woods to fall upon the orifice of the fruit" (18). Mickey Sabbath rifles through his best friend's daughter's underwear drawer and masturbates to her photo while he is a guest in the family home. Marcus Messner recalls, with a mixture of pride and chagrin, the day that Olivia Hutton gives him a hand job in his hospital room, she "sweetly" reciting the first lines of Longfellow's "The Arrow and the Song" as he ejaculates into the air (*Indignation* 130). And then, of course, there are the uglier scenes, also shot through with dark humor but difficult to laugh at: Portnoy attempting to assault Naomi in Israel in a bid to prove both his masculinity and his Jewishness; Peter Tarnopol, humiliated and emasculated by his wife Maureen, finally resorting to a physical fight and describing the image of Maureen covered in blood as "marvelous," the experience "euphoric" (*My Life* 280); David Kepesh describing his own "aggressive candor" that would more accurately be called harassment (*Professor* 123). These scenes are veritably brimming (sorry) with testosterone, alternately hilarious and infuriating, but invariably couched in a male character's fixation on his own masculine power and sexuality.

When people ask me perplexedly about my interest in Roth, I am sure they are thinking about scenes like these. I think they are wondering how I can spend so much time with literature that would for all intents and purposes leave me as an outsider. Still, even the most troubling or seemingly alienating scenes in Roth's fiction have never prompted me to dismiss his work, nor have they made the work feel exclusionary or inaccessible. In fact, my reaction has always been quite the opposite: I am compelled to look closer.

In a recent interview, after admitting that "there are some decidedly anti-feminist people" whose work she admires, author Chimimanda Ngozi Adichie was asked if Philip Roth was one of those people. She replied:

> Someone was telling me recently that they felt bad for liking Philip Roth. That bothered me. There was a humanity in Philip Roth's work that is often overlooked when we talk about his misogyny [. . .] Maybe there are people who want Philip Roth's misogynists to die at the end of the novel so that they'll know misogyny is bad. But that would be a little easy, wouldn't it? The world is complex. People are not perfect.

People are not perfect. That, to me, is the beautiful, ugly, heartbreaking, complicated, irresolvable center of Philip Roth's work. To reduce Roth or his characters only to the behavior that makes us uncomfortable is to miss what is so important about Roth's writing. In fact, I would argue that such an approach misses not only the whole point of reading Roth, but also of *reading*.

I have no desire to be Roth's "apologist," in the sense that I do not ever aim to excuse or dismiss the problematic behavior of his characters. When I explain why I read Roth, study Roth, and teach Roth, I consider my response also to be a defense of Literature, and all it is meant to do. As Zadie Smith reminded readers in her own reflection on Roth, fiction "is a medium that must always allow itself, as those other forms often can't, the possibility of expressing intimate and inconvenient truths." Literature asks us, as readers, to face the uncomfortable reality that people are messy, and to live with that truth—to struggle with it, to ruminate on it, to play both sides of hypothetical arguments about it in the middle of the night, knowing that we will never win either side—and to look for some element of humanity amid the ethical and moral chaos.

So much of Roth's own writing veritably begs the reader to find the humanity that Adichie also recognizes, even if at times it feels like a kind of perverse *Where's Waldo?* One of the most oft-quoted passages from Roth's novels issues this very plea, even as it describes the difficulty of locating anything concrete. "The fact remains that getting people right is not what living is all about anyway," says Nathan Zuckerman in *American Pastoral.* "It's getting them wrong that is living, getting them wrong and wrong and wrong and then, on careful reconsideration, getting them wrong again. That's how we know we're alive: we're wrong" (35). Zuckerman's words (an invocation in some respects of Samuel Beckett's "Try again. Fail again. Fail better" [89]) remind us that searching for humanity—in fiction, in the world, in an individual—requires accepting that no person has just one self, or just one dimension.

And so it goes with the sometimes frustrating and amorphous men in Roth's fiction to whom I keep returning, keep writing about and keep teaching about. We are set up to get these men wrong. One chapter captures their outrageous or offensive behavior and we find them unsympathetic or shallow or egotistical; the next chapter reveals the way their actions hinge on vulnerability and anxiety and suddenly we are not so sure; another consideration reveals that the latter doesn't eradicate or forgive the former . . . so were we right the first time? No, because a closer examination reveals some identifiable characteristic that mirrors our own lives, and certainly we aren't shallow. Are we? Part of Roth's gift is the ability to create these layers, subtly shaping an emotional depth to his characters that is never saccharine, critiquing his own flawed protagonists even as he draws them with affection.

The men in Roth's books, after all, do not receive their happy endings (in the sense of narrative structure, anyway), or even an ending at all in some cases—the joke on Portnoy, for example, is that after nearly three hundred pages, he has barely begun to understand himself, or the world, or his place in it. Peter Tarnopol quickly realizes that using physical violence against Maureen was not finally "marvelous" but "unmanning" (*My Life* 183). Mickey Sabbath reflects on the truth, once absurd to him in his youth but now all too real, that "you will evolve into a colossal schmuck more conscientiously than you can possibly begin to imagine, you will make mistakes on a scale you can't even dream of now—*because there is no other way to reach the end*" (*Sabbath* 396, italics in original). In *The Dying Animal*, David Kepesh confronts masculine anxieties exacerbated by age: "What do you do if you're sixty-two and you realize that all those bodily parts invisible up to now (kidneys, lungs, veins, arteries, brain, intestines, prostate, heart) are about to start making themselves distressingly apparent, while the organ most conspicuous throughout your life is doomed to dwindle into insignificance?" he asks (34). "I don't get any thrill trying to be a man," Charles Bukowski wrote in *Ham on Rye* (278), a line that might as well be a subtitle for any of Roth's books.

Yet Roth's work invites more than a distant sympathy, or a recognition of some vague idea about what constitutes "humanity." Instead, it invites a compassion that comes closer to empathy and identification. My life, in almost every way, could not be more different from that of Marcus Messner, but when I read the scene in *Indignation* where Marcus, to his increasing horror, is interrogated by the Dean, I think: somehow, I understand. I, too, have been consumed with frustration in the face of real and perceived injustice, have dug my heels in further, have left "such encounters scolding myself for the initial timidity and then for the unnecessary candor by which I overcame it and swearing in the future to answer with the utmost brevity any questions put to me and otherwise to keep myself calm by shutting my mouth" (*Indignation* 84). When I read Roth's descriptions of the concurrent horror and grief Coleman Silk experiences at being misunderstood, targeted, and made a pariah in *The Human Stain*, I think: somehow, I understand. Despite the significant differences in our experiences, Coleman's "moral suffering" whose "raw realism is like nothing else" feels palpable (12), and the ostracizing that results from an unthinking remark taps into a very real fear that I have certainly felt, particularly in an era when one ill-advised post on social media can be anyone's undoing.

I see how the resonance and reach of Roth's work manifests in other ways, as well, particularly among my students. I teach at a community college outside of Chicago, which draws a population of students from such different backgrounds that designing a syllabus that can "speak" to their varied range of experience and cultivate an appreciation for Literature is a daunting task. Early this semester—on the second day of class—I taught Roth's short story "Eli, the Fanatic" in an introductory English course. Not only had I just met these students on the day we discussed Roth, I had also made the decision to assign student discussion leaders for each text. Since the responsibility for shaping the conversation at the beginning of class resided with them, I walked into the class with little idea of what to expect.

The students only needed to hold independent discussion for fifteen minutes, but for the next thirty, I sat back and observed as they discussed this story among themselves, without any input from me, or any detailed historical context (that would come later). They spoke of anxieties about difference, fear of outsiders, and different definitions of what it means to be "American," ever-present issues that shape American society, perhaps now more than ever. Their sympathetic assessment of Eli Peck zeroed in on his sense of being trapped between conflicting elements of selfhood and culture; they hovered for some time on the relatability of his being deemed crazy for doing something that ran against the status quo. Later in the class, when we listened to a podcast about the recent tensions between white and Somali populations in St. Cloud, Minnesota—which led to white residents using zoning laws to prevent the construction of a mosque in the city—all of the students immediately recognized the connection to Roth's story, but no one was surprised. For all of the ways Roth's narrative might seem to render my students outsiders in terms of time, place, ethnicity, gender, and religion, their lasting impression was that of an undeniable familiarity.

"I read fiction to be freed from my own suffocatingly boring and narrow perspective on life and to be lured into imaginative sympathy with a fully developed narrative point of view not my own," Roth once said (*Why Write* 127). Roth's own novels provide the same opportunity to his readers, and in doing so, simultaneously offer a lesson not only in empathy and open-mindedness, but in patience. Aided by his unreliable narrators and a wry sense of humor woven into the fabric of his language, Roth asks that readers take a second and third look, that we reassess characters and circumstances, and question assumptions. In an age of diminishing attention spans and an increased tendency toward quick, oversimplified, unexamined, and divisive statements—modeled by America's own current president—Roth's work feels even more essential. Is it also "testosterone-y"? Sometimes. More than that, though, it is an incisive, hilarious, tragic, shocking, empathetic, ruthless depiction of our varied and imperfect selves. Maybe Roth would say I've gotten him wrong here somewhere, but that's living.

WORKS CITED

Adichie, Chimimanda Ngozi. "In Conversation: Chimimanda Ngozi Adichie." Interview by David Marchesa, *Vulture*, 9 July 2018. http://www.vulture.com/2018/07/chimamanda-ngozi-adichie-in-conversation.html.

Beckett, Samuel. *Worstward Ho*. 1983. *Nohow On: Three Novels*. Grove, 1995.

Bukowski, Charles. *Ham on Rye*. 1982. Harper Collins, 2002.

Roth, Philip. *The Dying Animal*. 2001. Vintage, 2002.

---. *The Human Stain*. 2000. Vintage, 2001.

---. *Indignation*. Houghton, 2008.

---. *My Life as a Man*. Holt, Rinehart, and Winston, 1974.

---. *Portnoy's Complaint*. 1969. Vintage, 1994.

---. *The Professor of Desire*. 1977. Vintage, 1994.

---. *Sabbath's Theater*. 1995. Vintage, 1996.

---. *Why Write? Collected Nonfiction 1960-2013*. The Library of America, 2017.

Smith, Zadie. "Philip Roth: a Writer All the Way Down. *The New Yorker,* 23 May 2018. https://www.newyorker.com/books/page-turner/philip-roth-a-writer-all-the-way-down

"The Book of My Life is a Book of Voices"

Philip Roth and the Bloodlines of his Fiction

Catherine Morley

The brio, the punch, the vigor, and the rich, rude tang of Philip Roth's writing have, of course, been well documented. In the innumerable news features after his death, critics, scholars, and friends reflected on the frenetic pace of his writing, as well as the humor, the vitriol, and the anger that informed his work. And surely not even the most skeptical reader can deny that Roth's prose throbs with a uniquely caustic and savage energy, which, as his friend David Hare has observed, was directed towards skewering hypocrisy wherever he saw it.

For me, though, the appeal of Roth's writing lies not just in its vigor and energy, but in its depth, its sophistication, its moral and historical profundity. People often describe his books as angry, funny, sexy, or moving; but I think the lifeblood of Roth's work is more than just an abiding wrath or lustiness. Rather it is his sustained engagement, throughout his career in fiction, with his ancestors, literary or otherwise. This energy manifests itself in two ways: in the raft of literary influences to which he was never shy of admitting, and in the various representations of characters who assess their lives in terms of those who have formed them.[1]

The first of these manifestations is nowhere more evident than in the book in which I first encountered Roth's distinctive voice, *I Married a Communist* (1998). Contemplating his life and the friendships that have formed him, an older Nathan Zuckerman reflects:

> What is it, this genealogy that isn't genetic? In my case they were the men to whom I apprenticed myself [...]
>
> [...] I became Leo's willing student, and through his intercession, Aristotle's willing student, Kierkegaard's willing student, Benedetto Croce's

willing student, André Gide's willing student, Joseph Conrad's willing student, Fyodor Dostoyevsky's willing student [...]

[...] the book of my life is a book of voices. (217, 221, 222).

It goes without saying, of course, that Zuckerman's sense of the multilayered intellectual ancestry informing his existence applies to Roth, too. And indeed, what immediately greets us when we open any of his books or short stories is a cacophony of voices, from Sheldon Grossbart's insinuations of brotherhood to Peter Tarnopol's feeling that his migraines give him a kinship with Virginia Woolf, from Merry Levov's revelatory stammer to the jump rope songs of Newark children's voices in *Nemesis* (2010). Every story teems with voices; every life is layered upon or shaped by relation to another; every text is buttressed by an intricate lattice of palimpsests.

One of Roth's abiding themes is the way in which we are shaped, for good or ill, consciously or unconsciously, by those around us: our friends, our communities, our families, our ancestry. A marvelous example comes in the story "Defender of the Faith," from the *Goodbye, Columbus* (1959) collection, which explores the relationship between Sergeant Nathan Marx and Lieutenant Sheldon Grossbart, retrospectively recalled by the older man. Nathan Marx, a hardened soldier (albeit also a thinker and scholar, in the very familiar Rothian combination of the intellectual and physical selves), finds himself in a training camp in Missouri in 1945, shocked to discover that he is a survivor of the war and annoyed by the overtures of an over-confident younger recruit who assumes an affinity between them, and cadges favors on the basis of their shared faith. As a thoroughly assimilated American Jew, Marx is forced to consider what he has sacrificed in pledging his allegiance to Uncle Sam. Throughout the story, he presents himself as having developed "an infantry-man's heart" (149) and rejects the attempts of Grossbart and his companions to establish a personal relationship. However, as he watches three Jewish personnel walking to their prayers, Marx yields to the gentle touch of memory:

> I could hear Grossbart singing the double-time cadence, and as it grew dimmer and dimmer it suddenly touched some deep memory—as did the slant of light—and I was remembering the shrill sounds of a Bronx playground, where years ago, beside the Grand Concourse, I had played on long spring evenings such as this. Those thin fading sounds. [...]

> But now one night noise, one rumor of home and time past, and memory plunged down through all I had anaesthetized and came to what I suddenly remembered to be myself. So it was not altogether curious that in search of more of me I found myself following Grossbart's tracks to Chapel No. 3 where the Jewish services were being held (157).

The story seems so simple, but its thrust is classic Roth: the impossibility of negating the past, one's memory, one's brethren. Indeed, Marx seems to admit that in order to know oneself, one must admit the double-time cadences of another. For as Grossbart's song grows more distant, so Marx's sense of his past grows closer. As the song fades, he realizes how important—how *decisively* important—the influences of his earlier life have been. Indeed, at one point in the narrative, Marx, for all his apparent antipathy to the Jewish soldiers at the base, realizes that he is defending the rights of Grossbart, Halpern, and Fishbein in their request for Friday night *shul* privileges.

Yet as ever with Roth, this apparently simple story is more complicated than it might first appear. Marx's search for himself does not simply deliver a forgotten Jewish past. He also comes to realize the ways in which his immersion in army life have shaped and disciplined him, thereby creating an uneasy tension with his Jewish self. This tension, this sense of in-between-ness, is exemplified in the scene in which Marx's commanding officer, Paul Barrett, upbraids Grossbart for asking for kosher food. Grossbart looks to Marx to validate his stories of illness and self-starvation; Barrett holds Marx up as an exemplary hero. Uneasily poised between the two antagonists, Marx perceives that each is trying to manipulate him for his own ends. "I felt like a Charlie McCarthy," Marx reflects, "with every top sergeant I have ever known as my Edgar Bergen" (151). The reference to himself as a ventriloquist's dummy, a puppet for the US army, is balanced here by Grossbart's repeated requests that Marx testify for him. And what the moment reveals, of course, is the way in which Marx has been formed by *multiple* voices, both Jewish and American. Armed with this knowledge and with a sudden awareness of the manipulation to which he has been subjected, Marx takes control of his interactions with Grossbart, and undoes the work the latter has engineered to ensure he does not get posted to the Pacific (a favor he had previously been imploring of Marx): "Behind me, Grossbart swallowed hard, accepting his [fate]. And then, resisting with all my will, an impulse to turn and seek pardon for my vindictiveness, I accepted my own" (184). The questions remain, of course: *who* is the defender of the faith, and *which* faith is being defended? For the truth is that Marx and Grossbart offer different kinds of Jewish American identities, with Grossbart at one point noting that "some things are more important to some Jews than other things to other Jews" (166).

But the theme that emerges most resolutely here—and one that Roth would go on to develop both formally and within the relationships embedded in his narratives—is the way in which all lives, all stories, are shaped by our forebears. Tellingly, where Marx and Grossbart come to bond is in an exchange regarding their parents. Each is a second-generation Jew; each has parents who continue to speak Yiddish and for whom Grossbart, at least, feels the need to speak (he feigns a letter from his father and protests that 'it is what my father *would* have written if he'd known how'). One obvious conclusion is that the story effectively demonstrates the ways in which second-generation American Jews negotiate a dual heritage. Yet I think the story offers something rather more visceral: a testament to the enduring power of ancestry and heritage. For when Grossbart holds his arm aloft to Marx, pinching the blue vein on his wrist, with the words "Blood is blood, Sergeant" (167), what he is emphasizing is precisely the importance of ancestry, not just in the obvious ways that form us, but in its role as the lifeblood of creativity. For whatever else he may be, Grossbart is also a fabulist.

While Grossbart insists upon the strength of blood ties, many of Roth's more memorable characters are far more indebted to the bloodlines of literary kinship than to those of genetic descent. Nathan Zuckerman's relationship with E. I. Lonoff in *The Ghost Writer* (1979) inevitably springs to mind, since it is here that Roth most fully articulates the idea of literary patrimony. In devoting himself to Lonoff, Zuckerman observes:

> I had come, you see, to submit myself for candidacy as nothing less than E. I. Lonoff's spiritual son, to petition for his moral sponsorship and to win, if I could, the magical protection of his advocacy and his love. Of course, I had a loving father of my own, whom I could ask the world of any day of the week, but my father was a foot doctor and not an artist [...] and I was off and away seeking patriarchal validation elsewhere (7).

But it is, perhaps, Peter Tarnopol who is the most audacious of Roth's writers in laying claim to a rich literary lineage. *My Life as a Man* (1974) revels in its own textuality, wallowing in the ways in which writers manipulate every inch of their materials, evident of course in the "NOTE TO THE READER," the "Useful Fictions," and "My True Story" which purportedly constitute the output of Tarnopol. "Salad Days" is particularly interesting here—who could forget the superbly named Sharon Shatsky and her deftness with a zucchini?—since it introduces the shift away from the bonds of blood.

Zuckerman—here the creation, it would seem, of Tarnopol—recalls his time at Bass College, his military service, his relationship with his proud father who beats him for messing around with a fishing hook, and his intensely Oedipal relationship with his mother. When Zuckerman leaves for college, the bond with his family is broken, his mother is replaced in his affections by the anglophile Caroline Benson, and the working class respectability embodied by his parents is replaced with a new second-generation intellectualism. One of the most interesting aspects of *My Life as a Man* is the way in which the narrator/speaker/Zuckerman/Tarnopol negotiates this shift into intellectual life. The art of fiction is seen as a means of self-revelation, and here the art of fiction entails a varied literary lineage. After Zuckerman (in "Courting Disaster," the second of the "Useful Fictions") makes off to Italy with his stepdaughter, a move he reflects upon as causing him to resemble Nabokov's "designing rogue" (69), and reflects upon his life with Lydia Ketterer, a figure who consolidates his rebellion from his family, he summarizes the relationship as follows:

> She saw the way out of her life's misery, and I, in the service of Perversity or Chivalry or Morality or Misogyny or Saintliness or Folly or Pent-Up-Rage or Psychic Illness or Sheer Lunacy or Innocence or Ignorance or Experience or Heroism or Judaism or Masochism or Self-Hatred or Defiance or Soap Opera or Romantic Opera or the Art of Fiction [. . .] I found the way into mine (96).

Zuckerman here offers the possible motives for messing up his life as a kind of multiple choice quiz, with the final possible answer derived from the title of an essay by Henry James. Indeed, throughout "Courting Disaster" Zuckerman conflates his own lived experience with past writers, texts and interpretation. We learn that Lydia has been the victim of childhood incest, but for Zuckerman incest is "an act I associated wholly with a great work of classical drama" (40), namely *Oedipus Rex*.

When he suffers migraines, Zuckerman sees the headaches as "*standing for something.*" He asks, "What did my migraines *signify*?" and explains his desire to find the cause of the headaches as down to a "literary habit of mind": "I could not resist reflecting upon my migraines in the same supramedical way that I might consider the illnesses of Milly Theale or Hans Castorp or the Reverend Arthur Dimmesdale" (55, italics in original). Dimmesdale is, of course, a character from Nathaniel Hawthorne's *The Scarlet Letter* (1850), Hans Castorp is the protagonist of Thomas Mann's *The Magic Mountain* (1924) and Milly Theale is the heroine of James's *The Wings of the Dove* (1902). To his satisfaction Zuckerman notes that Virginia Woolf had been regularly afflicted with migraines. But this leads him to wonder: "was I imitating the agony of this admirable writer, as in my stories I was imitating the techniques and simulating the sensibilities of still other writers I admired?" (57). Later still, Zuckerman likens his predicament to that of Joseph K in Kafka's *The Trial* (1925). Zuckerman's desire for literary progenitors is the stuff that makes the fiction, his story, so vibrant, so compelling and so paradoxically real. By citing all these forebears, not only is he insinuating a place for himself within a literary lineage, but he takes his story, a fiction within a fiction within a fiction, and somehow brings it into the world outside the text, imbuing it with a literary lifeblood with which it pulsates and quickens.

And so we return to *I Married a Communist*, a book within which Roth makes his most audacious bid to claim a literary progenitor.[2] The progenitor in question is William Shakespeare, whom Roth relocates temporally and geographically to the twentieth-century United States. *I Married a Communist* depicts the meteoric rise of Lincoln-lookalike Ira Ringold and his subsequent fall at the hands of his wife, Eve Frame, with the publication of her memoir "I Married a Communist" and the McCarthy witch-hunts. At one point Murray Ringold, one of the text's narrators and brother to the protagonist, meets Nathan Zuckerman while attending a conference that—in its title at least— registers Roth's literary ambition: "Shakespeare and the Millennium" (3). In effect, Roth is bringing Shakespeare to the cusp of a new millennium, both generically and thematically, in a tale of public betrayal, into which he weaves the themes and tropes of Shakespearean tragedy.

Indeed, Shakespeare does not merely inform *I Married a Communist*; he plays an explicit role within the text itself. As Zuckerman puts it, reflecting on his interactions with Murray Ringold, "I was being asphyxiated inside Shakespeare" (302). Fearful of possible suffocation, the narrator/writer further engages the tragedies for his own purposes, coloring them with modern historical specifications and inflections. In essence, Roth hybridizes the plays by making them relevant to the American national scene. In recalling the televised funeral of Richard Nixon, for instance, the narrator summons the words of Hamlet against Claudius: "Foul deeds will rise / Though all the world o'erwhelm them, to men's eyes" (279). But Ringold not only refers to *Hamlet* and *Macbeth*; he also invokes *King Lear* in describing the venomous Sylphid as akin to Goneril and Regan. As Zuckerman drives the decrepit, sleeping Ringold home after the tale has been told he, too, regresses to a classroom reading of *Macbeth*, a reinvention of Shakespeare in which the sleeping man, the storyteller, had assumed the roles of both Macbeth and Macduff.

There are, I think, few better examples of the literary bloodlines that animate Roth's fiction. His books are not merely monuments to the fizzing power of his prose; they stand explicitly in the shadow of his ancestors, both familial and literary. Like all great fictions, they are inhabited by the children of the author's imagination as well as the ever-present ghosts of his forebears. They are testimony not only to the immense resources of his talent, but to the enduring "brilliance of the deceased" (*Stain* 44).

NOTES

1. Many critics, have of course recognized and written at length about Roth's engagement with his literary forebears. The best example is probably Ross Posnock's important work *Philip Roth's Rude Truth*, in which he makes the case that "Roth has been

engaged in a lifelong conversation with canonical predecessors and contemporaries from Europe and the United States" (Posnock 7). Indeed, Posnock makes the case that Roth engages with the American Renaissance writers, by way of Henry James, as a way of confronting and revising models of rationality as set forth by Enlightenment philosophical models. See also Brauner (148-86).

  2. One might of course argue that it is in *Sabbath's Theater* (1995) that Roth first invokes Shakespeare as a precursor.

WORKS CITED

Brauner, David, *Philip Roth*. Manchester UP, 2007.

Posnock, Ross. *Philip Roth's Rude Truth: The Art of Immaturity*. Princeton UP, 2006.

Roth, Philip. "Defender of the Faith." *Goodbye, Columbus*. 1959. Penguin, 1986, pp. 147-84.

---. *The Ghost Writer*. Farrar, 1979.

---. *The Human Stain*. Vintage, 2001.

---. *I Married a Communist*. Cape, 1998.

---. *My Life as Man*. Cape, 1974.

Philip Roth
Face to Face

Ira Nadel

It was Chancellor Blvd. that brought me to Philip Roth. Stash's Anchor Inn on Hawthorne Avenue and the Weequahic Diner at the corner of Elizabeth and Hawthorne avenues also helped. My mother, Newark-born, would often return to visit her old haunts and I would troop along to enjoy a shrimp cocktail at Stash's or dessert at the diner. Often, we went shopping at Bamberger's department store for school clothes. In distant Rahway, the styles and choice were just not *au courant* for the suburban primary grades. My mother's preferred parking lot was next to the Empire Burlesque Theatre on Washington Street, a block from Market, and I vividly recall studying the posters of the scantily clad women just as Portnoy remembers in his complaint. The Adams Theatre, run by Harold Minsky, was another local attraction, but it was a few blocks away. The Empire and Adams, however, both had to close in 1957 because of new anti-burlesque bylaws. One night in January 1957, twenty-one of Newark's most talented performers were arrested.

South Orange, West Orange, and Irvington were not mythical but actual places for me with swim clubs, cousins, and even dates. Neil Klugman's world of *Goodbye, Columbus* was for me a place to touch and taste and linger. Connections with Roth existed even before I learned that he and I were both born in Newark's Beth Israel Hospital, although a decade apart.

I

Roth and I first met formally when I was an undergraduate at Rutgers (New Brunswick, not Newark). I soon began to read every new Roth work and vividly recall attending a seminar he gave for some fifty—or was it sixty?—at Princeton. Crowded into a large, oak-paneled room, I still remember his wry answer to what was back then an archetypal question: "do you write with a pen or with a typewriter?" He characteristically deflected a reply, choosing

Copyright *The Star Ledger*; NJ Advance Media. Published June 11, 1954.

instead to emphasize the daily struggle to write well, something borrowed from the world of Henry James, but expressed with Newark style.

My doctoral defense at Cornell unexpectedly continued my engagement with Roth. It was largely devoted to only one subject and it was not "Renunciation in the Works of Thomas Carlyle and George Eliot." *Portnoy's Complaint* took precedence, having appeared only a few months before. Of course, I had studied it carefully and considered myself a partial expert, confidently explaining to my New Jersey born committee member, M. H. Abrams, that it might indeed signal a new and enthralling urban Romanticism. He wanted to know more.

Roth after graduate school became a repeated pleasure, although I did not begin to write about him until years later. Articles, conferences, and a reference book expanded my own early understanding of identity politics for I, too, had spent listless hours in Hebrew School, wandered about Weequahic Park, and hoped to go to Bucknell—but Roth also taught me about the complexities of an American Jewish identity and conflicts with the social world one inhabited. Attracted to his language, themes, and carefully detailed settings, I sought to know more and his essays taught me what questions to ask.

Although there was halting correspondence over the years (most often with his legal representatives), we did not meet again until his eightieth birthday celebration at the Newark Museum. Offering congratulations while in the swirling crowd, he stared at me for a moment, aware I was about to undertake a critical biography, before saying, with a tone of incredulity, "You? You're Ira?" "Yes," I replied, unable to utter another word before he was swept away by his ardent admirers. I took solace in being photographed with Blake Bailey.

Without time for an incisive question, or another compliment that evening, I became an observer, understanding the importance of boundaries as he refused requests to sign books and even to speak to certain intrusive individuals. Roth was happiest entering with the Weequahic High School marching band and sitting with Edna O'Brien, protecting *her* from unwanted admirers. But he also gave the impression of a writer confident, in control and eager to experience even more than his eighty years permitted. In writing his life, I try to convey this energy, enthusiasm, and certainly good humor of a writer more at home, perhaps, with Hawthorne than Kafka, Twain rather than Bruno Schulz.

II

Roth's importance goes beyond that of a guide to what I and others like Mark Shechner recall of their Newark lives. This other Roth has become for many readers Roth the patriot and celebrant of the country of his birth, sometimes critical and sometimes not. This is the Roth who wrote "as a novelist I think of myself [. . .] as irrefutably American, fastened throughout my life to the American moment" ("Fallen" 335). Every sentence for Roth is an American sentence written in a vernacular immediately identifiable as American and inheriting the qualities of a Hawthorne, James, Bellow, or Malamud and who, on 9/11, hung an American flag in his apartment window in New York. But it is also the Roth who wrote *Our Gang*, his satire of Nixon, and who supported the protests against the war in Vietnam.

Roth's work is a history of contemporary America, his own rewriting of James's *The American Scene* (1905) or William Carlos Williams's *In the American Grain* (1925), although his real model is de Tocqueville's *Democracy in America* (1835). Growing up American is his persistent subject, blending with his Jewish environment, which surprisingly and unexpectedly provided him with the material of his early writing—prompted first by Richard Stern at Chicago and then by his first editor, George Starbuck at Houghton Mifflin, who shuffled and edited the stories in *Goodbye, Columbus* to emphasize their Jewish themes. Soon, Midwestern American life took over. From sixteen to eighteen, his earliest readings were works by Theodore Dreiser, Sherwood Anderson, Sinclair Lewis, and Willa Cather, later transferred to the worlds of *Letting Go* and *When She Was Good* ("Fallen" 332). For Roth, these authors expanded his geographic sense of America beyond "a Jewish neighborhood in industrial Newark" as he discovered what he poetically described as the "individual threads of American reality" ("Fallen" 332).

Passionately committed "to capitalize the L in life," he also worked to discredit the overused label "Jewish American novelist" ("Interview," *Reading* 129). The term had no currency for him: "the epithet American-Jewish writer has no meaning for me. If I'm not an American, I'm nothing" (McGrath). "I know exactly what it means to be Jewish and it's really not interesting. I'm an American" he earlier told the *Guardian* in 2005, adding "I don't write Jewish, I write American" (Krasnik).

Conversely, American recognition mattered, from placing his archive at the Library of Congress to his being only the third living writer, after Bellow and Eudora Welty, to be included in the Library of America, even if he found their proofreading shoddy. The numerous typos he identified in their edition of *Operation Shylock* disturbed him. In a letter of 12 March 2012, he told the publisher Max Rudin that he couldn't even finish reading the book because of the errors. It was heartbreaking, he noted, especially for a writer who rereads his final galleys three or four times over to ensure there won't be a single mistake (Roth to Rudin).

Measuring his love affair with America is Roth's language. As he emphasizes in his essay on Aharon Appelfeld and Saul Bellow, while observing their excited and penetrating Yiddish conversation, he remained rooted in English—not a bad thing. "English," he explains, not only "points to and represents reality for me, it is in itself a real thing: the most real of real things. Nothing is more tangible. Life *is* English. I am a man of English made," the syntax and meaning echoing an Emersonian affirmation of a national and linguistic identity ("Yiddish/English" 329). He then proudly reminds his readers that "Herman Roth and Bess Finkel were Americans from day one," adding that "writing in English is the greatest ordeal my life has presented me," but "my aesthetic responsibility—the Mosaic imperative of the American novelist—is to the English language" (329).

And it is this, Roth's language, with its exuberance, idioms, registers, and range that captivates readers beyond the travails of Alex Portnoy, Mickey Sabbath, Nathan Zuckerman, or even Simon Axler. Roth's multiple voices establish an orchestra of sounds, each distinct, like the unusual performers in his short story "On the Air," who audition before a talent scout. Reading Roth is reading language that alternately displays capaciousness and probity mixed with phrases and slang that always ring true. And the precision of his language matches the precision of his life. From the beginning of his writing career when he instructed his publisher concerning the advertising copy needed for his first book, *Goodbye, Columbus*, to his exact instructions regarding what should happen at his Memorial Service, Roth sought to direct if not control. His Memorial instructions indicate not only who should speak and in what order, but the length of time allotted to each and the music to be played at the end: Gabriel Faure's *Elegie* in C minor, Op. 24.

This moment, however, is about endings, not only of Roth's life but of his career and his writing, where endings take on a lyrical dimension: think of the ending of *I Married a Communist*, when Zuckerman wanders to the open pasture at the peak of his hill to consider the stars. Then several nights later he thinks of all those who have died, from his grandfather to Ira Ringold and Eve Frame, and with repetition offers an encyclopedic summary of what their loss means: "There are no longer mistakes [. . .] There is no idealism [. . .] There are no falsehoods" (*Communist* 322). This single, lengthy paragraph builds up to a crescendo of what freedom exists when one dies and what one sees: "that universe into which error does not obtrude. You see the inconceivable, the colossal spectacle of no antagonism" (323). This symphonic ending itself concludes with a galaxy defined by stars that "are indispensable" (323).

The end of *The Human Stain* with its frozen lake, or of *Nemesis* with the eloquent scene of Bucky Cantor, not stunted by polio, magnifies the image of a graceful finish. Bucky is in Apollonian form, throwing the javelin with elegance and athleticism before his awed students in another lengthy, final sentence of repeated gerunds creating a poetic, yet monumental conclusion for Philip Roth, as much as Bucky Cantor:

> Running with the javelin aloft, stretching his throwing arm back behind his body, bringing the throwing arm through to release the javelin high over his shoulder—and releasing it then like an explosion—he seemed to us invincible. (*Nemesis* 280)

WORKS CITED

Krasnik, Martin. "Philip Roth: 'It no longer feels a great injustice that I have to die.'" *Guardian*, 14 December 2005, translated by Sarah Paisley. https://www.theguardian.com/books/2005/dec/14/fiction.philiproth.

McGrath, Charles, "Philip Roth, Towering Novelist who Explored Lust, Jewish Life and America, Dies at 85." *New York Times* 22 May 2018. https://www.nytimes.com/2018/05/22/obituaries/philip-roth-dead.html.

Roth, Philip. "I Have Fallen in Love with American Names." *Why Write? Collected Nonfiction 1960-2013*. Library of America, 2017, pp. 331-35.

---. *I Married a Communist*. Houghton, 1998.

---. "Interview with the Paris Review," *Reading Myself and Others*. Vintage, 2003, pp. 119-48.

---. *Nemesis*. Houghton, 2010.

---. "To Max Rudin," Letter (typed), 12 March 2012. Taylor/ Roth Collection, Box B-001210, f. 14, Rare Books & Special Collections, Firestone Library, Princeton University.

---. "Yiddish/English." *Why Write? Collected Nonfiction 1960-2013*. Library of America, 2017, pp. 327-30.

ARTICLE

Roth Memorial

Patrick O'Donnell

Arguably the most compelling final paragraph of an American novel, perhaps only second to that of *The Great Gatsby*, occurs in Philip Roth's *The Human Stain*, published on the cusp of the new millennium:

> I turned from the shore, once I was safely there, to look back and see if he was going to follow me into the woods after all and to do me in before I ever got my chance to enter Coleman Silk's boyhood house and, like Steena Palsson before me, to sit with his East Orange family as the white guest at Sunday dinner. Just facing him, I could feel the terror of the auger—even with him already seated back on his bucket: the icy white of the lake encircling a tiny spot that was a man, the only human marker in all of nature, like the X of an illiterate's signature on a sheet of paper. There it was, if not the whole story, the whole picture. Only rarely, at the end of our century, does life offer up a vision as pure and peaceful as this one: a solitary man on a bucket, fishing through eighteen inches of ice in a lake that's constantly turning over its water atop an arcadian mountain in America. (*Stain* 360-61)

"The only human marker in all of nature, like the X of an illiterate's signature": thus Roth's ironic acceptance of the unreadability—the sheer opacity—of the human and the possibility of ever relating "the whole story." Yet Roth's life-project was a prolific and relentlessly provocative attempt to do so, or at least to fill in as many of the blanks as he could, in the time that he had, through all of those flawed and stained narrators and protagonists who inhabit his novels, blind and blind-sided here, illuminated by visions pure and peaceful there. No American novelist I know of, with the exception of Hawthorne, understood how deeply riven with contradiction the "nature" of "human nature" can be. In charting its excesses and its limitations, especially in the realm of self-understanding, Roth lost a lot of friends and made a lot of enemies, members of either party unwilling to accept his scorn for familiar categories; a novelist of filiation, he had no time for affiliation. His satirical proclivities, his attraction to the scandalous, his comic outrageousness—qualities that both vie and correspond with the philo-sophical seriousness and the probative cultural and historical density of his fiction—have confused some and irritated others. At century's end, he cap-tures perfectly in *The Human Stain* the antinomies of our growing intoler-ance of our own deep imperfection, paired with our growing lassitude in the face of human corruption and violence. In this novel, Roth implicitly pro-tests against reductionism in all of its forms; he is an adversary of the binary, the all-too-easy separability of guilt from innocence and pure from impure that seems to have invaded every aspect of our contemporary Manichean existence in the difficult new century he anticipates, via Nathan Zuckerman, as he takes a last look at a Vietnam veteran alone, ice-fishing on a lake "that's constantly turning over its water atop an arcadian mountain in America." Nature, or the paradoxical snapshot of impermanent, ever-changing nature captured in this "whole picture," may offer a vision of purity against which the illegibility of the human can be marked, but the unreadability of the human stain viewed not as DNA but as "X," a cross-out or cipher, signifies for Roth our impenetrability and excess beyond any mappings offered by science, law, politics, or religion. In a designation that he would have imme-diately recognized and embraced, he was the most secular American writer of his time.

Roth was not interested in life as a singularity, but in lives as pluralities, alterities. Most Roth protagonists live at least two lives, and though we some-times have Nathan Zuckerman and David Kepesh to try to sort things out, they almost inevitably fall back on a recognition that the story they can tell is only half the story, if that. Thus they project in the mode of "this is what happened to the Swede Levov I knew, or the one that I can imagine knowing if I knew him at all, which I'm not sure I ever did"; "this is the version of Anne Frank who died in life but who returned to life in a novel." But double lives, unreliable narrators, and possible worlds do not make Roth a postmodernist, or even a modernist: in many ways, his fiction defies those categories. He was, sans the categories, a contemporary writer who charted the trajectories of complicated personalities across a writing career that lasted over fifty years and included twenty-six novels, (or twenty-seven, depending how you count the title work of *Goodbye Columbus*; or twenty-nine, depending upon what genre you view *The Facts* and *Patrimony* landing in, as they come from a novelist who seemed to take great pleasure in erasing the lines between auto-biography and fiction). Of these, six were nominated for the single best work of American fiction published in the last twenty-five years by a 2006 *New York Times* poll of writers, critics, and editors: there were only twenty-two works in total on the list. One might debate the lopsidedness of this, but one could also argue that the poll demonstrates how deeply Roth tapped into the sheer diversity, insanity, and occasional magic of American life in the latter half of the twentieth century and into the new millennium.

Like him or not, no one could ever say that Roth lacked courage in raising the ambiguities of contemporary existence. Human sexuality was often his subject. Early on, in 1969, the notoriously graphic scenes of masturbation in *Portnoy's Complaint* earned him the reputation of a writer who would flaunt, with a finger in your face, the boundaries of taste and sensibility. The novel, banned in Australia upon its publication as well as many American home-town libraries, came as something of a shock from a writer who had preceded it with such works as *Letting Go* and *When She Was Good*. These, along with the early stories republished in *Goodbye, Columbus* seemed to announce him as the realist heir to Saul Bellow, as suggested in a letter from Bellow to Roth that David Gooblar cites in his revealing assessment of the relationship between the two writers: "There aren't many people in the trade for whom I have any use. But I knew when I hit Chicago (was it 12 years ago?) and read your stories that you were the real thing. When I was a little kid, there were still blacksmiths around, and I've never forgotten the ring of a real hammer on a real anvil." That letter was written in 1969, surely before Bellow had absorbed *Portnoy* or had the chance to gauge the comic exaggerations and inflammatory provocations of this "tabooed" novel depicting male adolescent sexuality. The novel caused Roth plenty of trouble, but it would not stop him from exploring the male sexual conscious and unconscious in novels ranging from his parody of Kafka's *The Metamorphosis* in *The Breast* to the depravities of Mickey Sabbath in *Sabbath's Theater*.

Even with his first published work, *Goodbye Columbus*, Roth was immersed in controversy: his comic portrayals of middle-class Jewish life led some to label him as a victim of Jewish self-hatred, a charge that continued through-out his career. He never let up in his exploration of sensitive and highly politicized topics, whether sex, or race in *The Human Stain*, Jewish identity almost anywhere in his novels, the Middle East in *Operation Shylock*, the Holocaust in *The Ghost Writer*, the Vietnam War and domestic terrorism in *American Pastoral*, the Nixon administration in *Our Gang*, communism and fascism in America in *I Married a Communist* and *The Plot Against America*. Roth became increasingly disturbed by the political divisiveness of contemporary American culture, but his unhappiness with its ugliness and his engagement with the histories that inform it were overcome by his desire to confront it with the work of the imagination. About the latter, Roth had something to say early on that has only gained in resonance over the fifty-eight years since the publication of his "Writing American Fiction" in

Commentary. Confounded by the response to the violent death of two teenage girls in Chicago and the media circus that followed in the age of television, Roth wrote that:

> the American writer in the middle of the 20th century has his hands full in trying to understand, and then describe, and then make *credible* much of the American reality. It stupefies, it sickens, it infuriates, and finally it is even a kind of embarrassment to one's own meager imagination. The actuality is continually outdoing our talents, and the culture tosses up figures almost daily that are the envy of any novelist. Who, for example, could have invented Charles Van Doren? Roy Cohn and David Schine? Sherman Adams and Bernard Goldfine? Dwight David Eisenhower?

In the age of Trump, we may find this lament too mild by half, and somewhat naïve in the midst of our crushingly embarrassing historical moment. But it reveals the extent to which Roth, immersed in *his* historical moment, took seriously the plight of the novelist who is daily bombarded with the noisiness and mess of reality, and who is committed to making some sense of it all—and perhaps, occasionally, mindful of the possibility of a millisecond or two of the transitory vision of purity that the imagination might render.

In his fiction, Roth chose a number of different ways to confront the incredibility of contemporary reality as he saw it. The forms his fictions take have often led to misunderstanding in a time when parody, irony, humor, and satire seem weak or cynical responses to the stupefying and sickening actualities which those genres and rhetorics address. They are not the only forms Roth's fiction takes, but these have appeared at times as too complicit with the reality that they mock—absurdist or nonsensical or mere "literary" responses to the horrors and craziness of modern life. Roth was clearly concerned in 1961 about the "meager" imagination's capacity to address this reality ("actuality is continually outdoing our talents"), and it is arguable that he spent the rest of his career, after arriving at this early recognition of his lot in life as a novelist, finding ways to address the dilemma he believed confronted every contemporary writer. How to write? How to create a "counterforce" to the force of reality? How to engage with it without allowing it to overwhelm one's sense of identity, one's place in history, one's purpose as a writer? Roth raises these issues in his fiction not as problems to be solved, but as predicaments that offer variable modes of address, from the serious to the serio-comic to the parodic and the absurd. Alternative history, writer's block, the many identities produced by self-reflection, the fraudulence and alienation of the sole "I," the solace and betrayals of community, the disorders and illumination produced by violence—all this and more makes its way into Roth's fiction as the result of his career-long attempt to understand how the imagination and reality conspire and interfere with each other.

That he was not always successful in this attempt is indisputable. No novelist this prolific, with a career that lasted this long, could possibly always raise the bar. His personality, at times, got in the way; his need for recognition (the sad quest for the Nobel which he should have won for "the American trilogy" alone), his ego (or the ego that inhabited him—often the subject of his fiction), his iconoclasm, and his self-estrangement haunt the edges of his canon. But what is indisputable, to my mind, is the centrality of his collected work to American writing as it extends from 1945 to the present. He wrote of American life in those years in ways that are both deeply personal and deeply historical. He understood the many ways in which we are surrounded with and infiltrated by multitudinous conflicting narratives of our connection to each other and what goes on around us, yet how we are also solitary, alone, like Lester Farley fishing on a lake fed by the waters running off an arcadian mountain. He found our condition farcical and laughable and scandalous, yet deadly serious and always evocative of the better nature we might have imagined for ourselves, and the flawed natures with which we must contend. His work will remain essential to our collective understanding of what it means to be here, both a part of and apart from the history of the present.

WORKS CITED

Gooblar, David. "Lessons from the Master." *The Guardian*, 7 October 2005. https://www.theguardian.com/books/2005/oct/08/fiction.saulbellow.

Roth, Philip. *The Human Stain*. Houghton, 2000.

---. "Writing American Fiction." *Commentary*, March 1961. https://www.commentary magazine.com/articles/writing-american-fiction/

Last Words on Philip Roth

Timothy Parrish

Philip Roth is dead. Frankly, he's been dead to me since 2009 when he stopped writing. Our relationship was always transactional. He was a writer and I was his reader, a faithful one, I insist. Each of his last five novels I read in one sitting the afternoon they were delivered to my house.

Nonetheless, the official notification came as a shock. My wife broke it to me. Honey, she said, better give me your phone. You're going to need to stay away from it for a few days. She apparently had noticed how these past several years I kept eyeballing it for the news flash announcing the title of his latest work.

No one person copes with grief like any other. I've kept him as near as I can. My wife even gave her pillow over to Roth's last book, *Why Write?* Likely she's noticed me talking to it, though I have tried to whisper. The cover mesmerizes me. He doesn't look like he knows he is dead. He looks a little pissed. His narrow eyes would scare me if I weren't able to read his lips when they moved. Hey bub, can it really be I'm actually dead and cannot return but for your glance?!

Between us, it's always been the same story. Possession. It's all Roth ever wants with readers. Alone in my study, and several times on park benches in cities I prefer not to recall, I've been possessed by him, repeatedly, as my hands fiercely cling to the bound object from which his face seems to take me in at a glance. Can such joy ever end?

For the longest time, everything seemed so private. But for those aliases he used to draw me close—Zuckerman, Kepesh, the heroic self-conqueror, Alexander—it was just Roth and me. Even when I discerned in his shifting manner a vestige of James, a revenant that conjured Hawthorne, or the pleasant aroma of Proust, I knew it was clowning. Only Roth could hold me like that.

Truly, I prayed that our intimacy never end. Why should it? We both wanted it that way? Don't lose this good thing, he sometimes sang to me as I read, but something was always coming between us. Life, most obviously, though Roth insisted real life could only happen when I was reading him. I hate to admit it, but I was the weaker one. Roth was true. I'm the one who compromised the relationship. I couldn't keep our thing to myself.

Since he's dead, I may as well confess. I betrayed "us." The way we were together, I told others. He didn't let on that he knew, but his coyness could be maddening. I happen to masquerade as a Roth scholar. Seriously. I wear a Roth mask and ventriloquize the master. It's, like, my job. Nor am I the only one, which is fine. Why shouldn't he have others? I don't care how many readers he possesses. I'm not a jealous person. But Roth is. His view regarding the mask was, and is, presumably, it's his alone to wear. And he had his ways of getting the message across. Shots across the bow. Warning missiles.

You remember when that famous English critic confessed Roth sat on her face while she read him? She didn't mean he used his living body, more like the time-space continuum was something he could negotiate at will. Her committee gave him a prize for it. I didn't celebrate. I understood Roth's gesture. The author had issued a gag order. Stop telling lies about me or else. I resolved to quit writing about him. But then a question occurred to me. Or else what? What could Roth do to hurt me except die? I happened to know he was in great shape because I knew a guy who knew a guy whose kid babysat for Roth's physician. He had ten years left, easy. That meant three, maybe four, more books. I kept my mask and used it only on the down low.

The next thing I hear he's telling the *New Yorker* he's finished. Quits. Didn't he understand I had to eat, too? Usually, I didn't even mean what I said when I talked about him. To protect our secret, I employed the abstract language familiar to other Roth masqueraders. Words like "Jew," "American," and the less controversial one, "novelist," were convenient, though I well knew he preferred they not be strung together consecutively in reference to himself. He wanted people to think he didn't care what we said about him, but he couldn't fool me. A writer who contrives to get himself into the Library of America before he is dead wants to live on. Like everybody else, though, he'll have to take what he gets.

Don't think he doesn't know it. Last night I took *Why Write?* in my hand as Hamlet once did Yorick's skull and asked him how his future looked now. His lips were surprisingly easy to read. "History claims everybody, whether they like it or not," he said and turned away. I saw through him, though. He was saying his death need not come between us. That explains the warm glow I felt on the morning after his passing. He had never seemed closer. Reading *The Dying Animal* was like old times. Better. It had a sweetness I had never known, which I chalked up to the fact that he was dead and I wasn't. I was feeling positively dreamy when a San Francisco radio station had the gall to interrupt our bliss. They wanted me to share my Roth with strangers! Fat chance! From now on, just the two of us! Sadly, the next day something happened that revealed Roth, as usual, was right. History meant to roll the both of us over, no matter what.

I was in my office organizing my library when a knocking stopped me. The future was at my door—it took the form of a student whose name I have forgotten. She asked what I was doing. Distracted by the many rings encrusted on her various fingers and most particularly the silver one shining from her nose, I shrugged and showed her the book in my hand—*The Cambridge Companion to Philip Roth*. You know students, they can floor you with a question. Hers was a doozy. Who is Philip Roth? Before I could answer, she hit me with another. Is he worth reading?

Right then I should have pressed into her hands *The Ghost Writer, Goodbye, Columbus*, maybe *Everyman*. My body betrayed me. My countenance blushed the shade of red Irving Howe is said to have experienced upon his legendary first reading of *Portnoy's Complaint*. Initially, I thought the glow from *The Dying Animal* was returning, but this flush was something different, something beyond Roth and me. In her expectant face, I saw that day, not too long distant, when readers would exist who could not enjoy the privilege granted to me—to have lived during the time Roth lived, to have known the joy of encountering a Roth novel on the very week or day it was released, to know even that when I'd read the book one, two, three times in succession, thinking, oh no, *it's over*, I could still nourish the sweet consolation that another entirely new Roth novel was already begun and would be arriving in due course. To me, Roth had seemed *inexhaustible*, a *living monument*. To her, he was just another dead guy on the shelf. How could she ever know Roth—live with him—as I had? Yet, she was the future—the coming generation of unknown readers who would, ultimately, put Roth in his place. From fear and, I admit it, loathing, I trembled.

My thoughts returned to that awful spring six years ago in Boston when I had gone to the ALA's annual ball for Roth Masqueraders. A dreadful, liminal time. We had just learned of Roth's self-inflicted retirement. We were in shock. His *oeuvre* had been arrested, forever. Only four of us appeared. The other masqueraders had gone to other rooms wearing masks I did not recognize, faces of Jews who had not yet surrendered their careers to eternity. From down the hall their laughter reached the room and disturbed our silence. Thirty minutes passed before anyone could speak. Had we only killed him ourselves, Miriam said, this day wouldn't be so hard. In moments of extreme stress, people are not responsible for what they say. We had been thrust into a dystopian future where no readers were left but us and the books we remembered all had the same thing written on their spine, Philip Roth, and no more were forthcoming. Soon we would have no choice to look backward, to find, or create, Roth's place in history. His life, in a sense, was in our hands. We were his critics. It was our task to bury him. Not that day, though. We couldn't face it. We thought it better to wait for him to die on his own.

One precious time I touched his living hand. He had just given a reading at the university where years earlier I had first read him as a student. He was so tall! I had to crane my neck to face him! He had just completed *Operation Shylock*. I was finishing my dissertation. Upon being introduced, I stammered like a schoolgirl. I asked about Emerson or Ellison, I forget which. He said something illuminating and then, kindly, asked about my project. I told him its subject was the logic of American literature, from its beginning to its end, and that my final chapter would address his work. He smiled and looked into my eyes as if he could see through them to the chapter that I had not yet written. I trembled in expectation of what he might tell me. When he finally spoke—the tension was almost unbearable—it was a question. "Say, you know your fly is wide open?"

I was so charmed by the Newark I fancied I could hear in his voice that several moments passed before the import of his words hit me. Then he turned to introduce me to his wife, a marvelous actress, who paid no discernible attention to my awkward, fumbling hands. I can't remember what happened next. Roth's question had already been seared into my consciousness—he remains the only genius I have ever personally known. I suppose his words have never left me. My fly is firmly fastened as I compose this *petit essai*.

Now it's the student's gaze that unnerves me. Modesty prevented me from disclosing a *personal acquaintance* that until now I have shared with no one else. Cursing my stupid silence, I turned abruptly for a book from my Roth shelf. When I turned to present the book to her—I had happened upon *The Dying Animal*—she was gone! Fate, however, had accomplished its purpose through her. I knew that henceforth my life would play out as a *Roth survivor*. It was my task was to remember—to answer her questions which lingered in the air—until my *kind* had passed from the earth.

You will notice from the space between paragraphs that I have had occasion to pause. In fact, several weeks have passed since the previous paragraph was finished and this one begun. Though I know perfectly well "what Roth means," I am reluctant to dish just now, and not only because the image of his succubus-like form suffocating my face as I write causes me to shake—with dread, yes, but also a tingle of anticipation. If you must know, my reluctance to continue is not to prolong this moment but a consequence of my suspicion that Roth is occupying the space between my own words. It is known, for instance, that between the time of his retirement and his reported death Roth miraculously entered the internet in order to controvert false impressions being gathered there in regard to his work. Freed from the necessity of writing fiction each waking day, Roth found himself surfing online and was stopped by his own Wikipedia page, whereupon he saw that others were doing to his life what he had once done with it too. They were making fiction of it—and, worse than that, making fiction of his fiction too. Resorting to his lawyer in the hopes that these alleged Roth experts could be stopped, he received from Wikipedia the following reply: "I understand your point that the author is the greatest authority of their own work, but we require secondary sources." One wonders who this "I" is. Roth says a Wikipedia Administrator, but the internet is mysterious, the nearest thing we know to heaven. Couldn't it be G-d asking Roth if he thinks he possessed the power to create himself alone? Whatever the case, my point is that, although expired, he may not have left the internet, which would mean, along with the Russians who are also said to admire him, he has access to my laptop.

Strange dreams afflict me. Recently, I have been seeing his corpse among worms, perhaps the very ones who once tried the virginity of Marvell's coy mistress. And I'm one of the worms eating him! Doubtless these dreams come from Roth. He's warning me to knock it off. Who am I, *a mere secondary source*, to declare who he was or what he meant? I'm one among legions! What can I know of the Roth who may endure?

Calm down, I tell myself, Roth can't be in everybody's laptop all at once. You won't be Roth's last reader. Roth assigns this task to History who may look like that student, in which case who knows what will happen with him.

It hardly seems fair. Anyone may say History is this or History was that, but why should History, whatever she looks like, get to say what Roth's place is when Roth worked so damned hard to write it himself?

Barring redemption, neither Roth nor I will know what History says he was. Honestly, I'm glad I'm not his last reader. I wouldn't want to tell anybody what he means. Christ, I don't know which word fits him better—Jew or American. My private guess, based on everything that has happened since the Hebrew Bible, is that Jews will last longer than Americans, not that my opinion matters more than yours.

Roth, ever Roth, forbade from his funeral the devotional rituals of his Jewish forbears, preferring to assert the utter annihilation of death. Of course he did! Death can't change that he's a writer and writers must go it alone. But if that's the case, why is he looking at me like that?

Roth, I whisper, so as not to wake my wife. Calm down. It's too early for definitive pronouncements. Can we leave it at this?

I'll die waiting to read your next book.

Contemporary American Literature, 1933-2018

Or, the Life and Progeny of Philip Roth

Aimee Pozorski

On the last Tuesday of September 2018, I had the honor and privilege of gathering at the New York Public Library, along with four hundred other admirers, to honor the memory of Philip Roth. Many folks who attended belonged to the New York literati—they move in circles in New York and had little to do with me. Hermione Lee was there from Oxford and Mia Farrow, Roth's neighbor, so I knew I was not the only resident from Connecticut. When I arrived at the private gathering in a torrent of rain, so Rothian, really, to let the weather speak our moods, I had to give my name to a young lady at the door. "Aimee Pozorski," I said, a little nervous. What if I wasn't on the list?

"Yes, there you are," she said politely and then ushered me through closed double doors leading to the grand Celeste Bartos Forum in the Stephen A. Schwarzman Building of the Library. Just moments earlier, I came up from the underground subway to breathe in the rain on 42nd street, and entered this New York institution like a sewer rat. But I was there for Roth, to honor his work and also his life, wondering how I had ever been invited in the first place—from whose list I had been plucked, invited with plenty of notice, as if Roth himself were there to oversee the arrangements.

In fact, he kind of was. As multiple speakers made clear that night, Philip Roth had been planning his own memorial service since the death of Saul Bellow. He revised the list of speakers a few times, but his closest friends and confidantes remained on the program. The final list included Claudia Roth Pierpont, Norman Manea, Bernard Avishai, Nicole Krauss, Janis Freedman Bellow, Judith Thurman, Julia Golier, Edna O'Brien, Andrew Wylie, and Ben Taylor, whom I had met before at Roth's home in Connecticut. Only Krauss wasn't able to make it, due to a family emergency. My husband joked that I, too, could have stayed home, given all that was going on in our family life. And yet, I wouldn't miss it.

When I heard of Mr. Roth's death, I was awake in the wee hours of the morning preparing to drive to Boston to fly to San Francisco for a series of academic panels hosted by the Roth Society at the national convention of the American Literature Association. I read the headline after it buzzed on my phone, felt the shock, thinking, as we all did, that Roth would live forever, and boarded a plane to fly three hours back through the time zones on a flight that would take six.

By the time I had arrived in San Francisco, I had voice mails from six reporters and had unexpectedly been quoted by the *Washington Post*, from an earlier interview I had done, which was then picked up by papers around the world. I was shattered, shaken, jet lagged, and out of time in the sense of being disoriented, as I tend to be, by movements between the time zones. I walked among the sea lions on pier 39 in San Francisco, bellowing wordlessly as those creatures did. I was surprisingly shaken by grief for a man I had known for such a little time, and for so practical a reason: To organize books on his shelves after a renovation of his farm house in Western Connecticut, and later, to plan his eightieth birthday party.

As speaker after speaker during the September memorial observed, Mr. Roth was a dear friend and a celebrated writer, and it took some effort to separate the two. There was the Philip who would ask questions of your life, what you are working on, your child; the one who would show you precisely how to line up books in his attic, prepare a plum and water, and walk you down to his pool. Then there was the Philip who produced a body of work so immense and significant that he is often called the greatest American writer of his generation. For as long as I knew him, and knew of him, he was considered by many to be the greatest American living writer of our time.

After he died, after I was able to parse the personal Roth from the iconic Roth, my entire sense of what I had learned about the contemporary American literary canon shifted. I think it had to do with one of the questions a reporter asked the morning after: "There is a sense of a death of American literature now—the end of an era—kind of like when Picasso died, but for literature." On the one hand, such a sentiment originally rang hollow for me—what was this, some kind of trap to make me sentimental?—but, on reflection, the death of Mr. Roth was one of the few occasions on which that could be true. Let me explain, lest you also think I *am* being sentimental.

When I received my graduate training in contemporary American literature, we always understood the dates of the tradition to begin during or after World War II, marked by a shift in worldviews after the Holocaust; marked, particularly, by our sense that trusted institutions were broken. American writers absorbed and reflected that as well as anyone. There was some question, however, as to when the tradition would end: the significant years marking this tradition were 1945 to the present for as long as I was a doctoral student, when things seemed to be steady for a while, but then the 9/11 terrorist attacks happened, then the election of Trump, then, the death of Roth. All of these American moments would likely leave a significant mark on our literary tradition; indeed, Roth wrote about all of them in one form or another, even his own death, which he imagined in *Everyman*.

As the contemporary American canon shifted and progressed, so too did the *oeuvre* of Roth: March 19, 1933 to May 22, 2018. The death of Roth was the end of one era, one marked by a sense of American-ness on the part of the writers who set out to write the great American novel. The birth of Roth, 1933, the year we associate with German nationalism taking root in the election of Adolf Hitler, was the beginning of that era. What would it mean to say contemporary American literature began with the birth of one of the greatest writers America would ever know, and that it ended with his death: May 22, 2018—a death that followed his rage against the election of our current president, one foretold uncannily, some say, in *The Plot Against America* from 2004, one that he lamented in an important *New Yorker* interview months after the election.

This is not to say that there are not other wonderful American writers working today, writers who will extend the literary tradition in their own way. But I don't think it will be through novels that are exemplarily American. On the one hand, Mr. Roth was famously generous with his praise and mentorship, bestowing, as he did, the mantle of high letters on such authors as Nathan Englander, Nicole Krauss, and Lisa Halliday, among others. However, as the global world opened to us, and the iPhone generation shifted and came of age, it seemed as though new American writers are less interested in conveying Americanness as they are invested in writing from a global point of view, with access to cultures and perspectives from all over the world.

Roth, on the other hand, especially after moving back to Connecticut in the mid-1990s to begin *Sabbath's Theater*, wrote the contemporary American project, for all of its successes and failures, promises kept and promises broken, constitutional crises and American pop culture. When Mickey Sabbath wraps the American flag around his shoulders, we understand Roth wrapping up in it too, and he seemed—for all his disillusionment over the Vietnam War, the Nixon Presidency, and later, still, with Trump—committed to the project of writing America, to America, for America. And I wonder if that will be true in the same way for any writer of his caliber again.

As Avishai, Professor at Dartmouth, and Wylie, Roth's agent, both underlined at the service: Roth wanted to tackle in the American Trilogy significant turning points during the three most defining decades of our time. He had a plan, as with all other things, as with the memorial service itself. To write like that would mean to embrace the solitary life of the writer, one of toil, vision, and re-vision, dark days and momentary breakthroughs. It would take immense sacrifice, more than before. And it would require a solitary life.

As Norman Manea, Roth's longtime friend, an expatriate from Romania and Professor Emeritus at Bard College, reflected, Roth once adopted two kittens and had to give them up because they riveted him. They took up too much time. He couldn't get his work done. Roth had told me that story, too: in his version, he put them in the cellar to play, but kept hearing their cries, their calls. When he opened the cellar door, they were looking up at him, beckoning him, needing him, and that is why he gave them up.

But when Bernard Avishai followed Manea, he further helped us understand the stakes of the life of a solitary writer like Roth. It was not only kittens he gave up, but children too, and the domestic life in which he was raised that he so much cherished as a child. Then, one by one, as the speakers continued to arrive at the podium, the issue of the child became a motif: first Avishai talked about Roth asking him in detail what it was like to put a child to bed. And there, he recalled, after describing to Roth his own experiences with fatherhood, is an exquisite rendition of the Swede putting Merry to bed in *American Pastoral*. Janis Freedman Bellow, Saul Bellow's widow, reflected on Roth's mockery of the ideal paternalistic response: she must not drink too much alcohol during her pregnancy or the poor child would have to go to trade school. Judith Thurman, staff writer at *The New Yorker*, recalled watching Roth play with a young boy—making constellations for him on the ceiling in the dark—long after the adults had retired. Andrew Wylie recalled his young daughter's essay about taking a call from Mr. Roth—a teasing, meticulous rendering of who called, complete with spelling, and ending triumphantly with the stern reminder that Wylie himself must not call him back lest his sleep be disturbed.

And then there was Julia Golier, Professor of Psychiatry at the Mount Sinai School of Medicine, who had dated Roth through the mid-1990s and convinced him both to publish *American Pastoral* after Roth had doubts as well as to keep his coveted farmhouse after he became determined to sell. To think I never would have met him had he sold that house—had he downsized the bookcases or moved just a town over—made me gasp a little at the question of alternative histories. I had known he dated a psychiatrist, that they were a private couple, but I had never seen Dr. Golier in an academic setting. To see her there on the platform of literary dignitaries was to understand Roth as the private man that he was: there, before all of us, was a former lover nearly always hidden from the limelight, blinking back tears as she described how she spent her life with Roth in quiet reflection, and, later, her decision to move on. After committing to establishing a family of her own, Dr. Golier ultimately met her husband and had twins, a daughter and a son. The son is the young boy for whom Roth made constellations. The daughter was his pen pal I had learned about earlier. She was writing now, Dr. Golier remembered her daughter saying, and wanted to trade drafts with Mr. Roth as email pen pals. When the two wrote a self-referential story about a pack of monkeys, Dr. Golier became concerned, saying he had gotten to her daughter, too. There he was, at the end, Dr. Golier said, the man who had become a grandfather without fathering children of his own.

I don't know why, of all of the luminaries there to remember Roth, it was Julia Golier's testimony that stayed with me. It has to do, probably, with the thought of what she gave up, a public life that she said she didn't miss, through his sacrifices, but also about what Roth gave up too, in the name of his calling: a family of his own, a mind at rest, privacy, personal commitment. Elisa Albert famously wrote in a short story addressed as a letter to Roth that she would have his prodigy child—and what a talent she would be, Albert fantasized— and here before me was a woman who gave birth to a young writer who would be Roth's adopted granddaughter but never progeny in the way we think.

A look back at the many essays I have written on Roth in the last fifteen years reflects a single, undying interest in the figure of the vulnerable child in Philip Roth's fiction, suggesting to me in new ways that, within his exemplary canon, maybe the child is more than a metaphor after all. Perhaps my obsession with this figure emerges from my teaching of contemporary literature, a course in which I ask students to consider common characteristics of contemporary American literature. One of those shared characteristics is the figure of the vulnerable child. Perhaps there remains, still, a vulnerable child within the most successful writers. Even still, I have always understood this universal investment as having something to do with our twentieth-century age of genocide, and now, in the twenty-first century, our anxieties in the age of terror.

I have long felt the need to read Roth in this way, both to understand Roth's emphasis on vulnerable children throughout his career—not simply as a gratuitous way to advance a plot, but rather as a way of presenting a consistent model for ethics in the twentieth century otherwise marred by humanity's failure to protect children from genocide, hunger, disease, homelessness, poverty, and abuse. Hearing his closest friends and colleagues speak of him in fatherly terms, in terms of the father without a child, reinforced this understanding for me—but now it goes beyond the figure of the child and considers what, for him, having a literal, physical child might mean.

Roth's focus on the child who is the victim of history has been a driving principle of his work since the beginning of his career. Roth's 1959 story, "Eli, the Fanatic" dramatizes the tension between the law, on the one hand, and the philosophy of ethics, on the other hand, with the story's protagonist ultimately choosing ethics as evidenced by his identification with a displaced Hasidic Jew and the orphans he seeks to educate near the story's end. A similar relationship between the orphaned child of history and the home can be seen in *The Plot Against America* (2004), which focuses its final eighty pages on the orphaned child, Seldon Wishnow. As Roth says in an essay titled, "The Story Behind The Plot Against America":

> the deepest reward in the writing and what lends the story its pathos wasn't the resurrection of my family circa 1941 but the invention of the family downstairs, of the tragic Wishnows, on whom the full brunt of the anti-Semitism falls—the invention particularly of the Wishnows' little boy, Seldon, that nice, lonely little kid in your class whom you run away from when you're yourself a kid because he demands to be befriended by you in ways that another child cannot stand. He's the responsibility that you can't get rid of.

We might also look back to *Letting Go* (1962), a novel about vulnerability and failure in the face of social and marital pressures that remain today. Given the dual plot of *Letting Go*, focused as it is on a man who marries young and struggles to please his wife while another continues to date amidst a burgeoning career, it would seem odd that it ends with such a focus on the fragility of the lives of small children. Then there is the surprisingly vulnerable child in Roth's 2009 novella, *The Humbling*. When readers first think of this book, they probably first think about Pegeen and the green dildo; second, they may think of Simon Axler, the failed actor—a kind of reverse Mickey Sabbath—who, by the novel's end, kills himself: perhaps the best performance of his life. But the first third of the novel takes a significant interest in Sybil Van Buren, a fellow patient at Hammerton and, particularly, her plight as it relates to her daughter Alison. It is in a conversation about the sexual abuse Alison suffers at the hands of people who should know better that Simon says: "People become infected with the rage when an innocent child is violated" (24).

The way children function as figures for something larger is clearer in some texts than others. I can see how the disenfranchised African American boy who likes "heart" books might be an alter ego or counter-self to Neil, the protagonist of "Goodbye, Columbus" (1959). The children in *Nemesis*

(2012) are all crucial to questions Roth raises about a disease attacking a whole community's children—and the same can be said for the homeless orphans in "Eli."

But there are other children who seem much less central to the plot or themes of the novels they are in. I once made the mistake of saying to Roth that the death of Markie *in Letting Go* is plain "gratuitous"; and that is not to mention the small child (unnamed) strapped to a toilet, a mess of shit and tears, that we are confronted with for multiple pages at the end of that loose, baggy novel. Further, why do we learn Faunia Farley's children have burned to death in a terrible accident for which she may or may not be responsible in *The Human Stain*? What could possibly be the purpose of such figures? I propose they signal a frustrated sense of a loss of futurity—not a loss processed in the sense of Roth's never having children in his personal life, but a loss in the more historical sense: in the sense that, since the middle of the last century, when Roth came into his own as a writer, history seemed to be working not for but against the disenfranchised and vulnerable.

Through these figures, Roth seems to ask: If we don't take care of our children, then what does that say about us as a culture—never mind our status as superpower or watchdog of the world?

A couple of months into my shelving work at Philip Roth's, I got brave enough to ask the famous author about the gossip I had been hearing since becoming President of the Roth Society. Among my questions were: is it true he had an affair with Nicole Kidman while working together on *The Human Stain*? (the answer is no); is it true he does not have children of his own—or, conversely, are there Philip Roth love children in the world who have sworn never to talk about their secret patriarch? Possibilities I had imagined are progeny with such famous and beautiful celebrities as Mia Farrow, Ava Gardner, Claire Bloom or, who knows? Maybe even Jacqueline Kennedy. The question of Roth's children had been weighing on me since it is one nearly everyone asks. Amy Nutt was the most recent, in 2013. A Pulitzer Prize winning journalist, she wanted to know of Roth's progeny—as everyone does.

The answer Roth gave me to the question of his children was not as straightforward as the Kidman answer—No, no, not with Nicole; but she is a lovely girl. Instead, he joked: Yes! Children! Of course! Brad Pitt is my love child with Nicole Kidman. Bringing us back full circle to the idiocy of most of the rumors surrounding him, Roth wove together the narrative of the Kidman affair with that of his mysterious children. That his love child would be none other than Brad Pitt, the charming, and rather dull, pretty boy would be the least likely candidate for Roth's child.

I offer this anecdote to point up 1) people's undying curiosity about Roth's children—either the fact of their possible existence, or the impossibility of them—increasingly now that we all have a hard time thinking about a world without a piece of him in it; and 2) Roth's self-consciousness in the face of such questions. He, too, must have heard the question many times before. He, too, must have thought about it as his friends gave life to families of their own, and their families had families too. Is there another way so natural for understanding a sense of futurity in the face of an aging talent like Roth's?

As Claudia Roth Pierpont argues of *The Humbling* in her recent book of interviews with Roth:

> There is no older or more familiar trap in reading Roth's work [...] than to mistake a book's voice for the author's autobiographical confession. [...] while it's true that Roth did have a torrid affair in these years with a forty-year-old former lesbian, he survived it perfectly well, and they are friends today. It's also true that he began to think about having a child and consulted a doctor about genetic feasibility—but this was a little later, and with a different lover. [...] What is important is that the affairs were becoming shorter and more difficult to maintain—just like the books. (311)

Provocatively, Pierpont seems to conflate Roth's personal life with his novels—as if the books themselves could metonymically shift to signify children, and relationships—both equally difficult to maintain. Even so, she too seems to believe in the possibility of a Rothian canon underwritten by the Rothian child.

Could an atheist American writer who lived a solitary life, who—in the end—had no children of his own, be the exemplary contemporary American author—and the representative of all of us who claim to value work, God, family, and freedom? Well, yes, of course. It is not the presidency, after all, and even if it were, I cannot imagine a better-loved leader than Roth. But I am struck, now, in hindsight, by the value of children in his work—the vulnerable but also brave, the sick and healthy, weak and strong, meek and aggressive, athletic and nerdy, reflective and articulate. For all of its emphasis on inter-generational conflict, the figure of the child, indeed, the presence of the child, seems central to our understanding of the new generation bursting forth, rejecting the apparent stasis and conservatism of their parents' generation. In Roth, we have that figure too—in Sheldon, and young Philip, and Merry, and the children on Bucky Cantor's playground, and the youngest daughter of the Patimkins who shows Neil the cherries in the basement fridge as early as 1959.

And we continue to have him, a father of writers who was so generous with his time in the end. He gave life to a new way of thinking about the American novel, about the life of the writer, about the fluidity and flexibility that is our American democracy. As everyone gathered together at his memorial reflected, in one way or another, we are better for having known Roth as a man and also for knowing Roth through his work. Late into the evening, we sat quietly, saying our personal goodbyes, while listening to a classical piece Roth loved, Gabriel Fauré's Élégie in C Minor, op. 24. On his deathbed, Wylie tells us, Roth whispered to him: "You have to let me go." Wylie says it was the hardest thing he ever had to do for Roth, the most difficult of his demands. In one sense, we must do the same—we must let him go. But we will always have his work, his children, his America, and, above all, his contemporary American literature: 1933-2018. Philip Roth.

WORKS CITED

Pierpont, Claudia Roth. *Roth Unbound: A Writer and His Books*. Farrar, Straus and Giroux, 2013.
Roth, Philip. *The Humbling*. Houghton Mifflin, 2009.
---."The Story Behind *The Plot Against America*." *The New York Times*, 19 September 2004, https://www.nytimes.com/2004/09/19/books/review/19ROTHL.html

Getting People Wrong

Some Preliminary Thoughts on Philip Roth's Passing

Matthew Shipe

A few weeks after Philip Roth's death this past May at the age of 85, I was invited to participate in a podcast hosted by fellow Roth Society member Danny Anderson. He had invited me on his show, *The Sectarian Review*, to discuss Roth's long and distinguished career and speculate on his ultimate impact on American literary culture. I had never done a podcast before and have always been apprehensive about the platform—when using it, I always recall that bit in David Foster Wallace's *Infinite Jest* (1996) when a Skype-like invention creates a sort of national existential crisis as people become pain- fully self-conscious and purchase attractive mannequins to be their stand-ins for video chats. Nevertheless, I was more than happy to talk about Roth with Danny and his other guest Michial Farmer, a friend I had met through Updike circles.[1] For around two hours we bandied about our favorite bits of Roth's work and somehow tried to solidify our thoughts on what his fiction had meant to us. Midway through the podcast, Danny and I recalled the *Roth@80* event, laughing at the memory of finding ourselves in a room with Don DeLillo, Nicole Krauss, Jonathan Lethem, Louise Erdrich, and, of course, Roth himself, without a drink anywhere in sight. The night was somewhat surreal—it felt a little bit like being thrust, sober and slightly underdressed, into a Fellini film.[2] I do remember managing to nudge myself in line behind Don DeLillo as he ordered a Sprite.[3] I think I ordered one too hoping that I might impress him (shockingly, the gesture wasn't noticed). At the end of that night, I made my way to the front of the room to talk with Roth—again, I'd like to reiterate that this would have been the type of event where a drink (or two) would have been very handy. It was my one time to meet Roth: I can't remember what I had told him—something fairly generic about how much his work had meant to me—but I'm grateful that I was able to tell him this and he was gracious in our brief conversation. As I was finishing up, some family friends approached and a flurry of pictures were taken. I like to believe that I'm in the back of one of those photos, an unidentified curly-haired mystery man never to be identified in some Roth family photo book.

After sharing stories of that night, Danny asked us to read aloud our favorite passage from Roth's fiction as a way to wrap up the conversation. While there are countless passages I could have selected, the choice for me was fairly easy. I turned to my well-worn copy of *American Pastoral* (1997), the novel that was my first real introduction to Roth when I was an undergraduate back in the late '90s. I qualify it as my "real introduction" because I know I had read a few of the stories in *Goodbye, Columbus* (1959) while in high school—we did "Defender of the Faith" and maybe "Eli the Fanatic" sometime during my senior year—but I had not really experienced Roth until *American Pastoral* was assigned in Professor Marshall Boswell's junior seminar titled "The Literature of Replenishment."[4] That course, more than anything, propelled me down the Roth rabbit hole. After the semester, I snatched up a remaindered copy of *Sabbath's Theater* (1995), and soon after found myself quickly making my way through much of Roth—zipping through the first Zuckerman trilogy after graduation, reading *Letting Go* (1962) after my first year in grad school,[5] and then tackling *The Human Stain* (2000) the summer after it had been released as I was recovering from that first year in grad school. I confess I didn't pick up *Portnoy's Complaint* (1969) until much later in my Roth reading, and I still haven't read *When She Was Good* (1967), a lapse that I was loudly called out on by students when that book was name-dropped in an episode of *Girls* (the episode of *Girls*, it should be said, was pretty good).

Yet *American Pastoral* remains the one Roth novel that I keep returning to—it creeps into my writing in moments when I least expect it and I find myself frequently citing passages in seemingly unrelated class discussion. Next to *Absalom, Absalom!* (1936), where I have marked nearly every sentence as "VITAL!" or have put a large question mark by it, *American Pastoral* stands as my most marked-up book, its pages filled with my largely illegible scribbling. When I teach it, I still use the paperback edition that I purchased in college, and the various annotations—some done in blue highlighter, later markings in red or black ink—offer fascinating evidence of how I have engaged with the novel for almost twenty years. The passage I ended up reading for Danny's podcast appears fairly early on, as Nathan Zuckerman recounts his final meeting with his childhood idol, Seymour "Swede" Levov. Zuckerman appears confounded by how little substance there now seems to be within the former high school athlete, a conclusion that spectacularly collapses when he later finds out what had actually happened to the seemingly charmed life of "Swede" Levov during the late 1960s. Reflecting on how he had utterly misread his boyhood hero, Zuckerman unleashes what remains for me his greatest diatribe, as he mourns the utter impossibility of really understanding another person:

> And yet what are we to do about this terribly significant business of *other people*, which gets bled of the significance we think it has and takes on instead a significance that is ludicrous, so ill-equipped are we to envision one another's interior workings and invisible aims? Is everyone to go off and lock the door and sit secluded like the lonely writers do, in a soundproof cell, summoning people out of words and then proposing that these word people are closer to the real thing than the real people that we mangle with our ignorance every day? The fact remains that getting people right is not what living is all about anyway. It's getting them wrong that is living, getting them wrong and wrong and wrong and then, on careful reconsideration, getting them wrong again. That's how we know we're alive: we're wrong. (35, italics in original)

The astonishing problem of other people, the endless impulse to grapple with the unknowability of even our closest friends and family, remains central to the argument that Roth pursues throughout not only *American Pastoral*, but also so much of his later fiction. Zuckerman exposes the seemingly insatiable need to figure out our fellow human beings despite the knowledge that we will, at best, always get them slightly wrong. This realization of our limitations—the knowledge that living is simply getting people "wrong and wrong and wrong and then, on careful consideration, getting them wrong again"—is not so much a nihilistic conclusion regarding our ability to exist as social creatures, but instead a sort of celebration of the very human need to try to figure each other and ourselves out.

Embedded within this perspective, however, is a potent argument for fiction's necessity as a vehicle for understanding ourselves and the frequently strange world we inhabit. The "lonely writers" may not—and probably do not—get it any more right than the rest of us, but the impulse to speculate, to play and get it wrong, that they embody is perhaps the most human of all responses. "All I can tell you with certainty is that I, for one, have no self, and that I am unwilling or unable to perpetuate upon myself the joke of a self," Nathan Zuckerman playfully declares to his English wife, Maria, at the end of *The Counterlife* (1986), the book that initiated the remarkable late career run that propelled Roth through the 1990s and the beginning of the next century (320). Zuckerman's declaration of independence from selfhood is partly postmodern bravado, but it also signals the necessity of fiction—playing with different voices and registers; spinning out outlandish scenarios for why things might have happened a certain way—in navigating the social world and carving out an identity. It's a vital argument for fiction's utility that courses through so many of Roth's novels. The fictions we produce are probably no closer to the truth than any other way of perceiving the world, but they are vital for capturing the contradictions and tensions that define our existence.

What remains remarkable about *American Pastoral* and the novels that followed it is how Roth transforms the problem of knowing other people into the equally knotty question of how we understand history. Roth's reconsideration of our recent history in his later work does not so much offer us a clearer or more accurate view of that past, but it instead illuminates the various myths that shape our historical narratives and exposes how we are vulnerable to the circumstances of history. In an often-cited passage from "My Uchronia," an essay he published before the release of *The Plot Against America* (2004), Roth articulates the argument that runs throughout so much of his later fiction:

> And now Aristophanes, the clown who must surely be God, has given us George W. Bush, a man unfit to run a hardware store let alone a nation like this one, a man who has merely reaffirmed for me the maxim that informed the writing of all these books and that makes our lives as Americans as precarious as anyone else's: *all the assurances are provisional*, even here in a two-hundred-year-old democracy. We are ambushed, even as free Americans in a powerful republic armed to the teeth, by the unpredictability that is history. (344-45, italics in original)

The "precariousness" of American life is in many ways the central subject of so much of Roth's later work, as he began to reflect on the changes that had radically transformed American culture during his lifetime. Again, these historical fictions do not expose the "real" past, but they illuminate just how fragile our existence, and our democracy's existence, has always been. That said, these later novels are not perhaps as pessimistic as this passage suggests. In *Exit Ghost* (2007), Nathan Zuckerman quells the impulse to comfort Jamie Logan and Billy Davidoff, the young writers with whom he watches the 2004 presidential election results come in. "It's a flexible instrument that we've inherited," Zuckerman tells a shell-shocked Jamie as Bush's re-election becomes a reality. "It's amazing how much punishment we can take" (82). Such reassurance does not assuage all fear—Roth's final novels expose just how violent life can be—but it does give a glimmer of hope for the future, suggesting the tenuous but resilient nature of American life. Happy endings, however, are anything but guaranteed, and Roth's novels—in all their glorious humor and devastating sorrow—remind us of how wonderfully and painfully brief our existence is. Fiction remains a necessary response for dealing with a world that more often than not confounds reason, and Roth's thirty-one books ultimately stand as a sustained gift that can helps us better appreciate how vital literature can be as we endeavor to comprehend ourselves and our nation.

NOTES

1. Slight confession: I'm also an executive council member of the Updike Society, and, if you happen to check out Danny's podcast (which you should), I should apologize in advance for all the Updike talk. The podcast can be found here: https://www.sectarianreviewpodcast.com/episodes-and-show-notes/episode-72-philip-roth-1933-2018

2. Danny may have made the Fellini comparison in the conversation.

3. A couple more memories worth mentioning: I remember Erdrich giving a very funny and slightly risqué toast to the birthday boy but can't recall the specifics of the toast. Late in the evening, I managed a semi-awkward conversation with Lethem as we were briefly on the same Dropbox account where Lethem and one of my college professors shared Dylan bootlegs. I was hoping that this would turn into a lengthy conversation on Dylan—where we might discuss vital questions, such as if *Infidels* contained "Blind Willie McTell" and "Foot of Pride," would it be his best post-*Blood on the Tracks* album? (it would be third behind *Love & Theft* and *Time Out of Mind*)— but the conversation took a swerve and we never quite got to have the great Dylan conversation I was hoping for.

4. Of all the courses I took at Rhodes College, this is the one that has stuck with me the longest, and its syllabus—John Barth, Don DeLillo, Toni Morrison, Jane Smiley, Rick Moody, Norman Rush, and Roth—has shaped my sense of post-1960 American fiction. I never finished Rush's *Mating* (1991), which, if memory serves, was the final book on the syllabus (sorry, Boz). I also didn't write on Roth, for some reason—I think I did my final essay on *The Ice Storm* (1994) and John Updike's *Couples* (1968). Pretty sure I got a B+ in the course, which was probably karma for not having finished *Mating*. Twenty years, and I still haven't finished that book (which isn't a slight on the book—I honestly don't remember much about it).

5. Credit again should go to Boswell as he was the one to suggest *Letting Go* as the perfect novel for the weird experience that is graduate school. He was right, but that is a subject for a very different essay.

WORKS CITED

Roth, Philip. *American Pastoral*. Houghton, 1997.

---. *The Counterlife*. Farrar, 1986.

---. *Exit Ghost*. Houghton, 2007.

---. "My Uchronia," *Why Write?: Collected Nonfiction, 1960-2013*. The Library of America, 2017, pp. 336-45.

ARTICLE

My Philip Roth

Debra Shostak

Halfway through a year I was devoting to writing a book about his work, Philip Roth appeared to me for the first time in a dream. He said little; in fact, he seemed interested only in talking to my husband rather than to me. He stayed on the fringes of the dream, looking sternly over at me once or twice, until the dream shifted away, as dreams do, and I was startled awake by the disappearance of my quarry. I was lying at my in-laws' house on a sofa bed, a rather inadequate contraption that slopes lumpily upward from your feet to your head, so you feel as though you should be rising rather than sleeping, restless, and guilty for your sloth. It was a Christmas in Wisconsin without snow, so desperately wished for by my children, like the outline of a story where the plot hasn't been filled in. That's how my dream felt, too.

Of course, I knew that it wasn't *Philip Roth* in the dream, it was me, or so psychoanalytic wisdom tells me, since it was my dream and not the real world in which I very nearly met the man I was spending all my days thinking about. But if Philip Roth *was* me, then my husband must have been me, too, which confusingly means that I *did* get to speak to Roth, though really I was talking inaudibly to myself and never heard his side of the conversation. I didn't meet Philip Roth in the dream, couldn't fill in the outlines that my waking imagination could color in just so far. Had I done so, I would have betrayed the fraught work of imagining subjectivities that Roth spent a career exploring, perhaps best captured in that riveting paragraph in *American Pastoral* in which Zuckerman confesses that "The fact remains that getting people right is not what living is all about anyway. It's getting them wrong that is living, getting them wrong and wrong and wrong and then, on careful reconsideration, getting them wrong again" (*Pastoral* 35). That, the writer admits, is the work of imaginative writing.

It's getting people wrong that is living. It's also the work of imaginative reading. That's what's so vital about reading, getting people wrong in all those ways that are right for us, at the moment and from wherever we are sitting. The experience of a dream is like the experience of reading a book, where we people the pages with our own resistant, three-dimensional images of the reality we know must exist, just as we know it. The beautiful wrongness of our reading depends on how reality is always slipping away from us, even as we form it into pictures and provocations and things that seem substantial until they aren't. Our subject—and subjectivity—when we read includes not only the "people" within the written world but also the person writing that world, and one of those persons is, well, me the reader, improbably decked out as an impersonation of the writer.

Of course, this is exactly what we literary scholars have scorned for years, ever since Wimsatt and Beardsley explained the intentional fallacy, and it is one of the first things we teach our students. Fiction is *not* autofiction, we assert; how naïve not to assume a stance of distance and detachment from texts that are only constructed storyworlds. Yet one might suggest that Wimsatt and Beardsley had to invent the fallacy because that is exactly what most readers do, and long to do; how else to establish a priesthood of readers? In any case, however obvious it seems when I express the thought, this notion—that we (rightly!) misread texts and others, and that among those texts and others we misread count the authors of our fantasies—has been one of the most intriguing, divertingly frustrating, enduringly pleasurable lessons that three decades of reading and rereading Roth have given to me, and much more forcefully and meaningfully than all the psychoanalytic and reception theories I've encountered to explain this project of intimate transaction that we call reading.

I never really met Philip Roth, except on paper, and while it has been one of my greatest disappointments, on reflection it may also have been my greatest boon in reading his work. In the late 1990s, I wrote him through his agent to ask if he'd be willing for me to interview him, because no scholarly interview had appeared since the excellent one published in Asher Milbauer and Donald Watson's *Reading Philip Roth* in 1988. He agreed—though only to conduct it in writing—but also with the proviso that he wasn't ready *that* year because he was absorbed in writing his current novel. I was to write him again the following year. I hopefully did so but was again deflected; by the time I saw the lovely *New Yorker* profile that David Remnick published in 2000, I decided that it wasn't meant to be. My thwarted attempt to talk—or "talk"—to Roth, however, seems a perfect allegory of reading. "We seek him here, we seek him there, / . . . That demmed, elusive Pimpernel" (Orczy 120). Roth, like any writer, is the spy in the house of fiction, the figure of Keatsian negative capability, taking on disguises so we only think we find "him." It would have been such a temptation to ask Roth my questions about his work. Realistically, so to speak (if one can ever speak of the reading experience "realistically"), I knew that any "confession" of his would, like the dizzying final assertion in the aptly titled "Note to the Reader" that concludes *Operation Shylock*, have been false (399). Arguably, of course, Roth has been leaving such notes to the reader throughout his career. So I found myself making up the answers, making up the man, having conversations in my head with a phantom. I invented parallel universes and a doppelgänger author who is my version of his version of who he is and is therefore also me. Thus my direct encounter with Pipik, one of Roth's most brilliant creations—an impersonation of himself, reversed in the mirror both literally and figuratively. He's the one that got away. That always gets away—so we keep reading.

I repeated my Roth-as-Pipik experience in two visits to the Roth collection at the Library of Congress in the mid-nineties and early oughts. I was thrilled to dig through the archive, especially because at the time the materials had not yet been thoroughly sorted and catalogued. The boxes that filled my order from an off-site location were liquor boxes. Cardboard liquor boxes! Yellow, white, and brown, sturdy or a bit ragged, Seagrams and Crown Royal, with the relevant novel title at times scrawled on a flap in Magic Marker in Roth's hand. I imagined these boxes being picked up from some local store near Roth's Connecticut home. Peering through the materials, I thought I saw Roth, or perhaps a trusted amanuensis, sorting the mess of drafts and notes for each novel into manila envelopes and separate boxes. I felt like Keats looking at Chapman's Homer and imagining Cortez's first view of the Pacific. Who has seen these things before? What is that frisson? I felt, too, like a member of Walter Benjamin's priestly classes, basking in the aura of an unreproduced and unreproducible art object. And even more so, in that I was looking at pages of notes in Roth's nearly illegible but absolutely distinctive hand, and at reams of typescript covered with deletions and revisions. The touch of the hand on pen or key; this is what I found myself yearning for. And why do I desire this? What do I think it will give me that I don't get even better from the worlds of the elegantly edited books? Some odor, or insight, some intimate entry to the mind behind the words? To make Philip Roth *me*.

We may pretend otherwise, but the reader's longings for an author seem to me essentially an erotic pursuit—the seductions, the deceptions, the abandonments; the illusion of union, of intimacy. We get picked up in the taverns of our own inner selves; writers feed us a line, get us drunk, and take advantage of us. This is why reading Lisa Halliday's *Asymmetry* (2018), for example, is such a tease, because she's doing a Rothlike performance, performing Roth himself, while the novel, never confessing the fact overtly, advertises it tauntingly for some 120 pages. Because the publicity for the novel coolly admits to Halliday's affair with Roth, his readers *want* the roman à clef, imagining on almost every page of the relevant section that we're meeting the clever, difficult, demanding prototype for the writer Ezra Blazer who—at last justice is done!—receives the Nobel prize, and also that we are in "Alice's" place (read: Lisa Halliday's), engaging in brilliant repartee—and sex—with the aging writer. In *Asymmetry*, Halliday, creating herself as an Alice in Wonderland, asks very Rothlike questions about fiction, specifically about writing as impersonation and illusion, exploring the mysteries of otherness, by way of a riveting, transgressive game that both invites and rejects our violations of a writer's privacy. She seems, like Roth, to have learned the lessons of the master (though his were Kafka and James). Like Roth, then, she also reminds readers that we're stalkers, who, like the quasi-psychotic Alvin Pepler in *Zuckerman Unbound*, reason that we've been invited into intimacy with the writer, who should therefore not be surprised that we're coming after him.

Roth knew that readers are as apt to *want* the writer as the complex world he invents. Thus his performance of irritation—succinctly expressed when "Philip" explodes at his partner in *Deception*, "'I write fiction and I'm told it's autobiography, I write autobiography and I'm told it's fiction, so since I'm so dim and they're so smart, let *them* decide what it is or it isn't'" (190, italics in original)—prickly, cagey, but denying nothing, really, and wickedly tempting further misreadings. Roth welcomes his delicious role as Wayne Booth's implied author extraordinaire. His intellectual come-ons to the reader appear not only, as one might expect, in the more overtly metafictional texts of his long, vibrant middle period, in which he anticipated "autofiction" well before it became a convention, but also in the more—seemingly—"realistic" fictions.

Just as Roth made capital during much of his career of the notorious attacks against his early work as not good for the Jews, so does he exploit the insistently autobiographical readings of his fiction by waving "Philip Roth" mockingly in front of his readers. We eagerly follow, from the storied misapprehensions about Alexander Portnoy as a Rothian id playing five-finger exercises on his instrument; to Peter Tarnopol, whom we're sure *must* have been married to Margaret Martinson Roth in *My Life as a Man* (and not to some "Maureen" or, as she appears in *The Facts*, "Josie"); to the many appearances of Nathan Zuckerman, whom Roth invites us to see as his alter ego throughout the *Zuckerman Bound* tetralogy and beyond, when he (Roth, or Zuckerman?) crafts the subtler but no less suggestive narrative framings of the American Trilogy and the final exit of Zuckerman's ghost, infatuatedly, pathetically conversing with a sexy young writer; to the terrorized boy in *The Plot Against America*, dependent on the towering strength of "Herman" and "Bess" Roth; on toward the artist who's "lost his magic" (1) in *The Humbling* and even, perhaps, to that suffering Everyman who humiliatingly longs for a last fling with an attractive young woman running in the park. As a reader, I'm game. I seek him here, I find him everywhere and nowhere. So much of the pleasure of reading is that see-sawing between immersion and awareness, the unique, convincing flavor of character and situation and the intimations of an author-self peeking out of every little crevice of the novel-dream. We write our authors, they don't write us.

The circularity of the reading experience, like that of my dream, drew me to Roth's fiction nearly thirty years ago. His work is peerless, and necessary, in its probing of dark corners of the American psyche and American history, its relentless inquiry into what it might mean to *be* an "American" (or Jew) in an inequitable pluralist society, its bravely ambivalent and perhaps justly nostalgic politics, its fearless exposure of the male id, ego, and superego—its conscience, that is, and penetrating moral vision that refuses conventional morality. Still, what I've most loved about Roth's writing is the hide-and-seek play that relentlessly, teasingly tests the reader's proclivities to think about *art*—about the manufacture of personalities in words, what Roth has called "the art of impersonation, [. . .] the fundamental novelistic gift" (*Reading* 143), and especially to seek the writer in the text even when we know we'll never find him. Nor should. This is why *The Counterlife* (the first of Roth's novels I ever read, and the one that hooked me) and *Operation Shylock* count among the works I most treasure, because of what they convey, so exuberantly, about how readers read.

We follow Nathan Zuckerman in *The Counterlife*, for example, through mazes of contradictory personalities, moving back and forth between disbelief and its suspension, always aware that Roth is having us on as he tears us from the narrative ground he's just placed our feet on. He tweaks us again and again, seeming to describe whatever we might call "reality" but really, to my mind, talking about how we perceive, and how words themselves are *all* that we perceive. Who else could have written this passage?

> The burden isn't either/or, consciously choosing from possibilities equally difficult and regrettable—it's and/and/and/and/and as well. Life *is* and: the accidental and the immutable, the elusive and the graspable, the bizarre and the predictable, the actual and the potential, all the multiplying realities, entangled, overlapping, colliding, conjoined—plus the multiplying illusions! This times this times this times this . . . Is an intelligent human being likely to be much more than a large-scale manufacturer of misunderstanding? (*Counterlife* 306, italics in original)

Listen to those sentences, their shape and balance and catalogues and delighted repetitions and oppositions, the plenitude and sinuosity, the confidence, the exclamation point and question mark, the insistence on meaning but only by way of form. Pay attention! Zuckerman the (literal) writer's writer tells us. Although Zuckerman is talking about an encounter in the novel's diegesis with Maria's anti-Semitic sister, his narrative jog through the meaning of Life—together with his reflexive description of the structure of the novel we're reading—makes the reader think we're hearing Roth's own voice, confounding the diegetic levels at which we position the narrating "I." And this is so even when at the last gasp he (Zuckerman? Roth?) brings us back to the present of storytelling, with Nathan situated within the action. "I didn't think so when I left the house," he answers his own question.

Or we get caught up in the hall of mirrors in *Operation Shylock*. Of course the Roth appearing at the beginning of the novel, suffering from his serendipitously named "Halcion madness" (*Shylock* 25)—for isn't the art of impersonation a halcyon madness?—*that* Roth is the man who writes the novel. We're sure of that because the author confirms the episode of psychological breakdown in *The Facts*, and we have to believe that we are reading the facts in a book published under that title, even though of course we get the joke, and even though the account appears in a letter that "Philip Roth" is writing with apparent seriousness to his character Nathan Zuckerman. Our compulsion to forget the transactions we are making with the writer and text may be as strong as the compulsion to pry off the masks, cleverly to pull the premise of verisimilitude to tatters—once and for all to distinguish the implied author from the real thing. So when the other Philip Roth appears on the stage of *Operation Shylock*, we at first smile with knowing skepticism but then get caught up in the action, as Tom Stoppard's Player cynically has it (23). Aren't we enticed to sign the contract the writer offers to the reader, and then, willingly, to forgive the writer's breaches?

What Roth has repeatedly reminded me, giving me great joy despite myself, is how any writer is a Pipik, and any reader is a Philip Roth sitting in that Hebrew schoolroom in Israel waiting for someone to show up, explain the mysteries, and tell him that he's neither lost nor foolish in his speculative reasoning and inability to read the letters—almost literally the writing on the wall—right before his eyes. And now, in mourning Roth's passing, I must accept that neither the elusive Pipik nor the explainer Smilesburger will ever reappear.

In a curious way, my tribute to Roth is like a "recovered" memory—a memory of what never happened but that feels more real than daily reality itself, insofar as it "happened" in the space of one reader's imagination. Hence the arrogant, appropriating folly of my title. My Philip Roth is the man behind the curtain of my most vivid, Technicolor readerly fantasies because in almost every book he teaches me what I do when I read, even as he makes fun of my doing so, and he does this by tempting me to invent him, fully fleshed and present, as the speaker of the words before me—only to realize that I may just be inventing myself. My point is to suggest that an inevitable part of the reading process is the intense and wholly imaginary relationship the reader takes up with the author, forever one-sided no matter how many layers of disguise we find ourselves trying to strip from the voices we read that refuse to talk directly to *us*. Peace be with you, Wimsatt and Beardsley. If I'm honest with myself, when I put on the mask of professional, critical distance, do I ever really escape the subject position into which a writer places me? Am I not, when I sit down with a novel and enter its storyworld, its only, and only intended, auditor? What is this secret pleasure, and why is it taboo? Isn't each novel written, really, just for me?

WORKS CITED

Halliday, Lisa. *Asymmetry*. Simon & Schuster, 2018.
Orczy, Baroness [Emmuska]. *The Scarlet Pimpernel*. 1905. Penguin (Puffin), 1997.
Remnick, David. "Into the Clear." *New Yorker*, 8 May 2000, 76-89.
Roth, Philip. *The Counterlife*. Farrar, 1986.
---. *Deception*. Schuster, 1990.
---. *The Facts: A Novelist's Autobiography*. Farrar, 1988.
---. *The Humbling*. Houghton, 2009.
---. *My Life as a Man*. 1974. Vintage, 1993.
---. *Operation Shylock: A Confession*. Schuster, 1993.
---. *The Plot Against America*. Houghton, 2004.
---. *Reading Myself and Others*. 1975. Revised edition, Penguin, 1985.
---. *Zuckerman Unbound*. 1981. Reprinted in *Zuckerman Bound*, Farrar, 1985.
Stoppard, Tom. *Rosencrantz and Guildenstern Are Dead*. Grove, 1967.

Contributors

Victoria Aarons holds the position of O. R. and Eva Mitchell Distinguished Professor of Literature in the English Department at Trinity University, where she teaches courses on American Jewish and Holocaust literatures. Her publications include *A Measure of Memory: Storytelling and Identity in American Jewish Fiction*, *What Happened to Abraham: Reinventing the Covenant in American Jewish Fiction*, *The New Diaspora: The Changing Landscape of American Jewish Fiction*, *Bernard Malamud: A Centennial Tribute*, *The Cambridge Companion to Saul Bellow*, *Third-Generation Holocaust Narratives: Memory in Memoir and Fiction*, and, with Alan L. Berger, *Third-Generation Holocaust Representation: Trauma, History, and Memory*.

Ann Basu lives in London. A former librarian, she is a researcher and writer whose interests are in modern English and American literature and the history of London. She gained a PhD from Birkbeck College, University of London in 2010. Her book on Philip Roth, *States of Trial: Manhood in Philip Roth's Post-War America*, was published by Bloomsbury in 2014.

David Brauner is Professor of Contemporary Literature at The University of Reading (UK). He is Executive Co-Editor of *Philip Roth Studies*, co-editor of *The Edinburgh Companion to Modern Jewish Fiction* (2015), and the author of three books: *Post-War Jewish Fiction: Ambivalence, Self-Explanation and Transatlantic Connections* (Palgrave/Macmillan, 2001); *Philip Roth* (Manchester University Press, 2007); and *Contemporary American Fiction* (Edinburgh University Press, 2010). His essays have appeared in a wide range of journals, including *The Journal of American Studies*, *The Yearbook of English Studies*, *Studies in the Novel*, *Modern Language Review*, *Canadian Literature*, *Studies in American Jewish Literature*, and *Studies in Comics*.

Alan Cooper, Professor Emeritus, York College, CUNY, retired from teaching in the spring of 2017. Notable among his numerous contributions to periodicals, reviews, and books is his *Philip Roth and the Jews* (1996). He is now working on *The Paskudnyak Trilogy + One*, a Young Adult satire on current life set seven hundred years ago.

David Gooblar is a Lecturer in the Department of Rhetoric at the University of Iowa. He is the author of *The Major Phases of Philip Roth* (Continuum,

2011), and the co-editor, with Aimee Pozorski, of *Roth After Eighty: Philip Roth and the American Literary Imagination* (Lexington, 2017). His next book, *The Missing Course: Everything They Never Told You About Teaching in Grad School*, will be published by Harvard University Press in 2019.

Jay L. Halio is an Emeritus Professor of English at the University of Delaware, where he taught both Shakespeare and Jewish American literature.

Patrick Hayes is a Fellow of St John's College, Oxford University, where he teaches literature in English from the eighteenth century to the present day. He is the author of *J. M. Coetzee and the Novel* (2010) and *Philip Roth: Fiction and Power* (2014), and the co-editor of *Beyond the Ancient Quarrel* (2018). He is currently working on a history of life-writing in the postwar period.

Brett Ashley Kaplan earned her Ph.D. through the Rhetoric Department at the University of California, Berkeley and is now the Director of the Initiative in Holocaust, Genocide, Memory Studies and Professor and Conrad Humanities Scholar in the Program in Comparative and World Literature at the University of Illinois, Urbana-Champaign. Her books, *Unwanted Beauty: Aesthetic Pleasure in Holocaust Representation* (2007) and *Landscapes of Holocaust Postmemory* (2011), examine the Shoah's intersections with art and space. Turning to race and power in contemporary Jewish American literature, she published *Jewish Anxiety in the Novels of Philip Roth* (2015) and has written the *Dictionary of Literary Biography* entry on Roth and articles for other venues such as *The Conversation*, https://theconversation.com/philip-roths -journey-from-enemy-of-the-jews-to-great-jewish-american-novelist-97151.

Michael Kimmage is a professor of history at the Catholic University of America. In 2012, he published *In History's Grip: Philip Roth's Newark Trilogy* with Stanford University Press. His next book, *The Decline of the West: An American Story* is forthcoming with Basic Books.

Pia Masiero is associate professor of North American literature at the University of Venice, Ca' Foscari. Her research interests span Nathaniel Hawthorne and the American Renaissance, Faulkner, and contemporary US and Canadian literature. Lately she has worked on the experience of reading and the mechanisms that trigger empathy using both second generation post-classical narratology and cognitive sciences. She is the author of two books: *Philip Roth and the Zuckerman Books: The Making of a Storyworld* (2011) and *Names across The Color Line: William Faulkner's Short Fiction 1932-1941* (2012).

Maggie McKinley is an Associate Professor of English at Harper College in Illinois. She is the author of *Masculinity and the Paradox of Violence in American Fiction, 1950-75* (Bloomsbury, 2015) and *Understanding Norman Mailer* (University of South Carolina Press, 2017), and her work has also been published in *Studies in American Jewish Literature, Philip Roth Studies,* and *The Mailer Review,* among other places. She serves as the Program Director for the Philip Roth Society and President of the Norman Mailer Society, and is currently editing a collection entitled *Philip Roth in Context* for Cambridge University Press.

Catherine Morley is Associate Professor in American Literature at the University of Leicester. She has published *The Quest For Epic in Contemporary American Fiction* (2009) and *Modern American Literature* (2012). She has recently edited *9/11: Topics in Contemporary American Literature* (2016) and co-edited *American Thought and Culture in the 21st Century* (2008) and *American Modernism: Cultural Transactions* (2009). She has written numerous essays on modern and contemporary literature and culture for journals such as *Journal of American Studies, Review of International American Studies, Gramma,* and *Modernist Cultures.*

Elèna Mortara taught American Literature at the University of Rome "Tor Vergata" and was a Fulbright Visiting Scholar at Brandeis and at Columbia. She is the author of a book on the first three centuries of Jewish American literature (*Letteratura ebraico-americana dalle origini alla shoà*, Litos, 2006) and of numerous essays on twentieth-century Jewish American writers. She also wrote on cross-cultural encounters in American literature. Her book *Writing for Justice: Victor Séjour, the Kidnapping of Edgardo Mortara, and the Age of Transatlantic Emancipations* (Dartmouth College Press, 2015) was awarded the 2016 ASN Book Prize by the European Association for American Studies. She is the editor of the Italian critical edition of Philip Roth, *Romanzi, Volume primo, 1959-1986,* Meridiani Mondadori, 2017.

Ira Nadel, Professor of English at the University of British Columbia, has published biographies of Leonard Cohen, Tom Stoppard, David Mamet, and Leon Uris, as well as edited *The Cambridge Companion to Ezra Pound.* His *Critical Companion to Philip Roth* appeared in 2011, and his lengthy essay "American Roth" will appear in 2019 in the *Fudan Journal of the Humanities and Social Sciences.* He has recently written on Virginia Woolf, Samuel Beckett, and Hannah Arendt, although not in the same essay.

Patrick O'Donnell is Professor Emeritus of English at Michigan State University. His most recent book is *A Temporary Future: The Fiction of David Mitchell* (Bloomsbury, 2015); he is currently completing a book on Henry James and contemporary cinema, co-editing *The Encyclopedia of Contemporary American Fiction 1980-2020*, and commencing work on *An Introduction to the Fiction of Thomas Pynchon* for the Cambridge University Press "Introductions to Literature" series.

Timothy Parrish edited *The Cambridge Companion to Philip Roth*. His nearly factual story, "Roth's Final Hours," appeared in *Raritan* two years before Roth's reported death. He is currently a Professor of Comparative Literature at the University of California, Davis.

Aimee Pozorski is Professor of English and Director of English Graduate Studies at Central Connecticut State University, where she has taught since 2004. She has written and edited books on Philip Roth, literatures of 9/11, and HIV/AIDS representation. She served as President of the Philip Roth Society from 2009-2015 and will begin her term as Executive Co-Editor of *Philip Roth Studies* in 2019.

Matthew Shipe is a Lecturer and the Director of Advanced Writing in the English Department at Washington University in St. Louis. He has published essays on John Updike, Philip Roth, Raymond Carver, Don DeLillo, and Barry Hannah. In 2015, he won *The John Updike Review*'s Emerging Writers Prize for his essay "The Long Goodbye: The Role of Memory in John Updike's Short Fiction." Alongside Scott Dill, he is editing *Updike and Politics: Due Considerations*, which is forthcoming from Lexington Press. He currently serves as President of the Philip Roth Society and is on the Executive Board of the John Updike Society.

Debra Shostak is Mildred Foss Thompson Professor of English Language and Literature at the College of Wooster, where she chairs the Film Studies program. She is Executive Co-Editor of *Philip Roth Studies*, the author of *Philip Roth—Countertexts, Counterlives* (2004), and the editor of *Philip Roth—American Pastoral, The Human Stain, The Plot Against America* (2011). She has published on numerous contemporary American novelists, such as Paul Auster, Jeffrey Eugenides, Jonathan Safran Foer, John Irving, Maxine Hong Kingston, and John Updike, and on film, with a special focus on cinematic adaptations. Her next book, *Fictive Fathers in the Contemporary American Novel*, is forthcoming from Bloomsbury in 2020.